Men of the Kingdom

Cyprian: The Churchman

By

JOHN ALFRED FAULKNER

Professor of Historical Theology in Drew
Theological Seminary

WIPF & STOCK · Eugene, Oregon

Wipf and Stock Publishers
199 W 8th Ave, Suite 3
Eugene, OR 97401

Cyprian
The Churchman
By Faulkner, John Alfred
Softcover ISBN-13: 978-1-7252-8475-3
Hardcover ISBN-13: 978-1-7252-8477-7
eBook ISBN-13: 978-1-7252-8476-0
Publication date 7/15/2020
Previously published by Jennings and Graham, 1906

This edition is a scanned facsimile of the original edition published in 1906.

CONTENTS

Chapter		Page
I.	Carthage and the Church,	5
II.	Conversion,	18
III.	Cyprian's Judgment of Heathenism,	26
IV.	A Pope,	36
V.	Before the Storm,	47
VI.	The Decian Persecution,	58
VII.	A New Question in Discipline,	74
VIII.	Cyprian, the Lapsed, and the Church in Carthage,	84
IX.	The Novatian Church,	102
X.	Mercy and Help,	122
XI.	The Lord's Prayer,	140
XII.	Cyprian, the Catholic,	147
XIII.	Was Cyprian a Roman Catholic?	163
XIV.	The Great Controversy with Rome,	176
XV.	The Crowning,	189

APPENDICES

		PAGE
I.	THE INTERPOLATIONS IN THE DE UNITATE ECCLESIÆ,	208
II.	CHRONOLOGICAL ORDER OF THE EPISTLES,	216
III.	SELECT LITERATURE,	219

INDEX, - - - - - - - 225

NOTE

Readers who wish to verify statements in this book, or to study further Cyprian's life and testimony, will please remember that in the references to his Epistles the numbering of the Oxford edition (followed by Hartel) is first given, and then in parentheses that of Migne (followed by the Ante-Nicene Library). In the case of a few of the Epistles the numbering is the same in both editions.

Cyprian: The Churchman.

CHAPTER I.

CARTHAGE AND THE CHURCH.

Sailing through the Strait of Gibraltar from the west, one passes Morocco on the south for about 200 miles, and then Algeria for 600,—both the ancient Mauretania, only the northern edge of which was taken possession of by the Roman Empire. A small Eastern section of Algiers was the province of Numidia, conquered by Rome B. C. 46 and entirely incorporated into the empire, in which was the town of Hippo Regius on the coast, about 120 miles directly west of Carthage, the seat of the bishopric of the greatest man God ever gave to the Ancient Church—Augustine. The eastern section of that high Algerian coastline until it turns directly south and runs south for 300 miles, is Tunis, ancient

Carthage, which, with part of Numidia and the coast of Tripoli, formed the province of Africa Proconsularis. Then the mariner sails on east a thousand miles till he comes to the famous city of Alexandria, 500 miles south from Carthage, separated on land by vast wastes. The reader will thus see how misleading our rough and ready designation of North Africa is in giving us a glimpse of ancient relations. The provinces of Egypt and Africa had no more to do with each other than India and Canada to-day. Egypt was imperial province, occupied by an army, and under the emperor's immediate control; Africa was a senatorial province, governed by one of the consuls chosen by lot.

Carthage was only one hundred miles from Sicily, which was the connecting link between Italy and the South. Its position made it of great importance to Rome. Who controls Carthage controls the Mediterranean, or at least goes a good way toward controlling it. So thought France, which in 1881 brought Tunis under her wing, and thus offset the possession of Gibraltar by England. No doubt war between Rome and Carthage was inevitable. There could not be two masters of the western Mediterranean. It is not necessary to give here the history of those fearful Punic wars, in one of which the greatest general in all history—a man against a nation—performed prodigious, apparently impossible, feats, and brought Rome to the verge of ruin. Suffice it to say that finally, B. C. 146, Carthage fell into Roman hands and like Jerusalem later, was razed to the ground. Twenty years after, Caius Gracchus tried to found a colony there but failed. Julius Cæsar saw the importance of this, but fell under Brutus's dagger before he could carry out his intentions. The first emperor, Augustus, however, succeeded in establishing a Roman colony on the site of Carthage, which in the third century when our hero came on the stage, was one of the chief cities of the empire.

The Carthaginians were Phœnicians or Canaanites. They were a Semitic race, but had none of the ennobling religious conceptions of their kindred, the Jews. They are an everlasting object lesson by contrast of what Divine revelation can do for a people. "Who made thee to differ?" They were one of the bloodiest and cruelest races of antiquity, and "their religion the most hideous ever practiced by a people emerged from barbarism." If there had to be a war between Carthage and Rome, it was for the infinite gain of the world that Rome was conqueror. But they were not exterminated; in the new Carthage they lived on with the Romans. But the city became Roman through and through: its baths, its games, its monuments, its pursuits. The Third Legion was quartered there, and great and useful works were executed under their supervision. That there was intermingling of blood there can be no doubt. But in any given case we can not tell exactly how the matter stood. Did Cyprian have Carthaginian blood?

It is not necessary to say that the Roman civilization which took the place of the Punic had its defects, yes, its fearful faults. It was also coarse, cruel, and licentious, though not in the same degree, and idolatrous, though without human sacrifices. What old Carthage was we can read in the tremendous novel "Salammbo" by Flaubert, who has gone into the conditions with minute and exhaustive learning. In the papers of the restive and tumultuous Carthaginian, Tertullian, a greater man than Cyprian, thought not historically so significant, we have a picture drawn from life of that civilization which came after. It is sufficient to read only one book—that "On the Shows." Pompey consecrated the theaters to Venus, and made them in a sense a temple. Other shows had been devoted to Bacchus. So, says Tertullian, we have these two evil spirits

CARTHAGE AND THE CHURCH.

in sworn confederacy with each other, as the patrons of drunkenness and lust. The theater is immodesty's peculiar abode, where nothing is in repute but what elsewhere is disreputable. So the best path to the highest favor of its god is the vileness with which the Atellan gesticulates. The very harlots are brought upon the stage. Let the senate, let all ranks blush for very shame. The tragedies and the comedies are the bloody and wanton, the impious and licentious inventors of crimes and lusts. If it is right to indulge in the cruel, the impious, and the fierce, let us go to the theater and games. Let us regale ourselves there with human blood.[1]

In a students' club of a German university I once heard one of the members highly laud old Rome, and say that a minister could not do better than to study the Greek and Latin classics, and take from them his models. How far the speaker was in solemn earnest, or how far he spoke in banter or bravado, I do not know. But for such a one a course in Tertullian would be an excellent discipline. There were redeeming features of course in the Roman. The Roman farmer worked and made every one who belonged to him work. But even here pagan hardness appeared, which left its im-

[1] De Spectaculis, chs. 10, 17, 19.

press on European civilization from that day to this. "Pliny saw him or his native tenent in Byzacium yoking an old woman with an ass, a practice not dropped till late." Is it dropped? I have often seen women harnessed to milk wagons, and sturdy girls helping the dogs pull home loads of clothes for Monday's wash. The Roman knew how to civilize in his way; he had a fine military and civil organization. He represented the majesty of law, to which Paul appealed, and under which the new faith made its way. But, as Archbishop Benson finely says, a "fearful shadow dogged all this national and individual vigor, the inherent vice of the Roman spirit, the scornful inhumanity with which uncivilized populations were unhelped and repelled. It was this, with its ever pursuing train of consequences, this and not the Vandals, which brought the last wreck."[2]

Who introduced Christianity into Carthage or when, we shall never know. When Cyprian meets us it was already widely established over Numidia and proconsular Africa. It was nothing to him to bring together fifty or eighty bishops. Doubtless numerous Christians came with the early colonists, and with the constant intercourse between Carthage

---
[2] Cyprian: His Life, His Times, His Work, XXVII, XXVIII.

and Rome, like that between Boston and Halifax, it was inevitable that an aggressive and attractive faith like Christianity would be widely represented. Africa was a second Italy—it belonged rather to Europe than to our Africa. Its literature was Latin. When the Church at Rome was a Greek exotic, its clergy, its literature, its language all Greek, the Church in Africa was Latin. The great African Tertullian opened Latin literature in the closing years of the second century before what we know as the Latin Church was born.[3] Africa had a Latin Bible before Rome—she was the mother land of Christian Latin literature, and in this, as Harnack says, she had a world-historical significance.[4] Far from being the teaching Church of the west, Rome for two centuries had not a writer of note, while in Tertullian Africa produced a writer of range, power, and fertility.

But Carthage, like Rome, had its Greek element. For the play lovers of his city Tertullian wrote his books on plays in Greek.[5] Her lovely and noble martyr, Perpetua, spoke Greek with Bishop Opta-

---

[3] It is not meant to deny the priority of Minucius Felix, which, in the opinion of many, Ebert has set beyond question; but, as a fact of large historical significance, the above statement stands. Harnack still holds that Tertullian was first.

[4] Mission und Ausbreitung des Christentums, Leipz. 1902, S. 515.

De Corona, 6.

tus and Presbyter Aspasius. The Greek translations of the oldest African Martyr Acts may be as old as the Acts themselves.[6] This Greek element, however, was not a preponderating one, as it was in Rome. Africa was the first Latin Church.

At any rate when the first historical notice of the African Church meets us in Tertullian we have a strong and wide-spread society. "Our numbers are so great," he says, "constituting all but the majority in every city. What will you make of so many thousands, of such a multitude of men and women, of every age and every dignity? What will be the anguish of Carthage herself, which you will have to decimate, etc.? Spare Carthage if not thyself."[7] As to the extent and influence of Christianity, Asia Minor was the only parallel. It had even gone among the original Carthaginians, though to what extent at the time of Tertullian and Cyprian we do not know. Probably not largely, as the names of the third century are almost altogether Latin. But among the martyrs there were Punic names— in fact, the first African martyr, A. D. 180, was a Pune. In the fourth century it was necessary, or at least very desirable, for the bishops and priests

---

[6] Harnack, Ibid. 514.

[7] Ad Scap., 2 and 5. Cf Apol., A. D. 197, chs. 2 and 37.

CARTHAGE AND THE CHURCH. 13

to know Punic, though there never was any Punic translation of the Bible. To the Punes the Bible was read through an interpreter, or they had their sermons in Punic.[8] But there was no Punic Christianity as there was a Celtic.

A most interesting fact is noted by Harnack, which may help us in our search for the origin of Christianity in Carthage. And that is the strong military element in the speech of the Church writers there. Not only in Tertullian, a son of a soldier, but more strikingly in Cyprian, where military language is almost standard and prescriptive. So also the large use of legal language, which can not be referred entirely to the converted lawyers, Tertullian and Cyprian. The Church speech, says Harnack, which was created in Africa, shows that, so far as it was not the common speech, it was the product of immigrant officials and military men.[9] Does not that mean that Christianity owed its origin and support in Africa, as elsewhere, in part to converted soldiers?

The greatest man in the African Church was Tertullian, and the greatest man in the Christian world of his age (say 155-230). He is well worthy

---

[8] See Zahn, Geschichte des Neutestamentlichen Kanons, I, 40-44. Harnack, Mission und Ausbreitung, 515.   [9] Ibid. 516.

of treatment in this series. Not a single life of him exists in English, except the old study by the learned Bishop Kaye (1826, 3d ed. 1845), and hardly an essay in the Theological Reviews,[10] though the Germans have a whole shelf of books on him. The greatest literary master of Church history in Germany, Professor Albert Hauck, of Leipzig, sprang into fame by his fine life of Tertullian in 1877. Tertullian was the watershed of ancient Church history, the turning point of primitive and Catholic Christianity. The Church owes a vast debt to him, because for her he wrote the strongest defense she had received up to that time—an apology of tremendous power and effectiveness. Then his little book "To Scapula," proconsul of Africa, is one of the noblest pleas for toleration ever made. In variety, strength, and volume of literary output he far exceeds Cyprian, and he always maintained a more genuinely Christian attitude. It is true that, disgusted with the worldliness of the Church, he later became a Montanist, and on account of this divergence from the so-called Catholic Church, which he criticised with relentless severity, the later Church omitted him from her roll of saints. Cyprian fed his soul on him. Some of his books

---

[10] But see J. B. Mayor in The Expositor, July, 1902.

are but the echoes of Tertullian. "Hand me the Master" (*Da Magistrum*), he would say to his secretary when asking for the rolls of Tertullian.[11] He said truly. Of all the Christian men who lived in the dying years of that fateful second century, Tertullian was the master.

I have already mentioned the large number of bishops in the African provinces. At a council, A. D. 240, ninety were present. That means a widely diffused episcopal organization, but no diocesan organization. In other words, every little town had its bishop,—and entirely distinct from presbyter, be it remembered. Of detached presbyters and deacons we hear nothing. Harnack says that the episcopal organization in Africa was formed on the model of the municipal organization there, which itself was derived from the Phœnicians. He quotes Mommsen to the effect that when Roman rule began in Africa, the Carthaginian country at that time consisted essentially of small city societies, administered by their suffetes, of which small city organizations there were about 300, and that Rome allowed that arrangement to stand.[12] And on that old Punic civic platform the Church imposed her already developed episcopate.

---
[11] Jerome, De Vir. Ill., 53.
[12] Harnack, Ibid. 516, note 5. Mommsen, Röm. Gesch. V, 644.

What circumstances contributed to make Christianity so strong in Africa we do not know. It may be because such powerful personalities as Tertullian and Cyprian were given to the Church. For a hundred years Carthage was the cynosure of all eyes. Cyprian stood forth like the governor of a province. In the middle years of the third century he and not the Roman bishop was pre-eminently the pope. Under him the number of converts among the heathen were greatly increased. "The new crowd of believers," he calls them.[13] Strong men are as necessary to impress heathens to-day as then. Piety is indispensable to a missionary, but it will not make up for brain power and learning. So Carthage was the central city of Christianity in the middle of the third century, and this was largely due to Cyprian. He corresponded with bishops in Rome, Spain, Gaul, Cappadocia; he looked to it that his letters on the lapsed should come to the notice of all the Church,[14] and he ruled the Church of North Africa from Syrtis to Mauretania.[15] And what that Church was is brought home to us by the estimate of Harnack that in proconsular Africa and near-by provinces there were about 150 bishops.[16] What if as strong men as Cyprian

---

[13] Ep. 66 (68), 5. [14] Ibid. 55 (51), 5. [15] Harnack, 517, note 2. [16] Ibid. 519.

had succeeded to the Carthaginian bishopric! Would Rome have won her supremacy so easily? And what if Vandal and Mohammed had not decimated the African Church! Might there not have been one large section of Christendom outside of the Roman "sphere of influence?"

CHAPTER II.

CONVERSION.

THASCIUS CYPRIAN was born we know not when nor where, but probably near Carthage in the early years of the third century. His parents were rich, and for a child of pagan parents only two professions lay open—arms or law, this latter including rhetoric. Like Tertullian he chose law, and in Carthage attained high standing in it. "He gained great glory to himself," says Lactantius, "by the profession of the art of oratory."[1] The lawyer and rhetorician of ancient times was supposed to be a master of all the sciences that then were. He had not only to know what to speak, but how to speak and to act, to be a master of grace as well as of reason. He had not only to be a man of learning, but to have his learning and every other accomplishment in readiness for the persuasion and convincing of men. The average modern lawyer would shine poorly by the side of the wide and persevering culture of the ancient advocate. At thirty Cicero

---
[1] Div. Inst. V. 1.

was still under the tuition of Molon. How persistent they were in technical perfection.[2] A rhetorician of Cyprian's time was so highly honored that his daughter was espoused to the Emperor Gordian. Is it any wonder that when such men as Minucius Felix and Tertullian and Cyprian were converted, they exercised immense influence on the higher classes?

Africa was the special "nurse of pleaders," reminding Archbishop Benson of the fervor and eloquence with which Ireland has "enriched the English bar." Not the least of them was Cyprian. He had pursued the highest culture of his time. "What gold, what silver, what raiment," exclaims Augustine, "he brought with him out of Egypt!" When Jerome wants to illustrate the greatest power of Christianity, viz., that of converting men of learning and culture, men "who are the last of all to learn the word, yet at length, like the Ninevites descend from their thrones to plebeian levels, lay aside the radiance of their eloquence, put away the intoxicating draught of words, and thenceforth content themselves with the majesty of Christian thoughts," he selects Cyprian as an example.[3] It was indeed a trophy for Christianity.

---

[2] Aug. Chr. Doc. bk. 4.   [3] Comm. in Jon. c. 3.

What about the circumstances of Cyprian's conversion? Alas! here we know almost next to nothing. But a careful study of Pontius's "Life of Cyprian" (Pontius was his deacon and friend) and of Cyprian's own letter to Donatus throws a little light. Pontius refers his conversion to the influence of Cæcilius, a presbyter, whose name he took in baptism, as Neander did the names of his friends. "He had close association among us with a just man of praiseworthy memory, by name Cæcilius,[4] in age as well as in honor a presbyter, who had converted him from his worldly errors to the acknowledgment of the true divinity. This man he loved with entire honor and all observance, regarding him with an obedient veneration, not only the friend and comrade of his soul, but as the parent of his new life."[5] But of this faithful soul-winner we know nothing more. He has vanished from the horizon of the Church, just as many another worker has done after bringing some one to the Savior who has been a burning and shining light. It was personal service, personal friendship, the strength and beauty of Christian testimony of the unknown Cæcilius, which gave us Cyprian.

In the letter to Donatus there is none of the

---

[4] Hartel's MSS. have Cæcilianus,   [5] Vita Cyp. 4.

intimate personal heart history which makes the confessions of Augustine so fascinating and so famous. There are striking figures but no clear soul-history, rhetoric but not much light. "While I was still lying in darkness and gloomy night, wavering hither and thither, tossed about on the foam of this boastful age, uncertain of my wandering steps, knowing nothing of my real life, and remote from truth and light, I used to regard it as a difficult matter that a man should be born again, a truth which the Divine Mercy had announced for my salvation, and that a man quickened to a new life in the laver of saving water should be able to put off what he had formerly been, and, although retaining his bodily stature, should be himself changed in heart and soul."[6] This shows that he became convicted of sin, so that his old life appeared in its right colors; and it shows also that he had often thought of Christianity and of its doctrine of the new birth. He then goes on to say that he came to acquiesce in a sinful life as inevitable, indulge his evil habits as "actual parts of me," until finally by the "help of the water of the new birth, the stain of former sins had been wiped away, and the light from above serene and pure had been in-

---

[6] Ad. Donat. 3 (Ep. 1).

fused into my reconciled heart, after that by the agency of the Spirit breathed from heaven a second birth had restored me to a new man; then in a wondrous manner doubtful things at once began to assure themselves to me, hidden things to be revealed, dark things to be enlightened, so that I was able to acknowledge that what previously being born of the flesh had been living in the practice of sins, was of the earth earthy, but had now begun to be glad, and was anointed by the spirit of holiness."[7]

By the instructions and example of Cæcilius he had gradually come to a knowledge of himself, and to a desire to become a Christian, and apparently at or after baptism his faith laid hold on Christ, and he was transformed into a new creature in Him.

It is evident also by the epistle of Donatus that another element contributed to his conversion, viz., the comparative purity of the morals of Christians. His association with Cæcilius and his observation of other Christians, was making hideous to him by contrast the pagan civilization in which he had been brought up, revealing it in all its cruelty, rottenness, and shame. For in this letter, a kind of confession, a kind of

---

[7] Ad. Donat. 4 (Ep. 1).

justification and explanation of his change, he devotes the chief space to a frank description of the heathenism he had left. "I will draw away the veil from the darkness of this hidden world." And he gives a picture of it as he knew it, and he knew it, this cultured wealthy lawyer of the great city. It is a picture that can well be commended to the admirers of pagan ethics and art, who think we could well exchange Christianity for Greek philosophy. There is no doubt that on the part of many Christians there was a sad lack, as we shall see, in showing forth the moral beauty of their religion, but at the worst the latter was so infinitely superior to paganism to the keen eyes of this observant and practiced lawyer, that he was unconsciously and irresistibly drawn towards it.

After these descriptions he pictures a soul freed from this bondage. Withdrawn from the eddies of a distracting world, he lifts his eyes to heaven; and, having been admitted to the gift of God, he can boast that whatever in human affairs seem lofty and proud, lies beneath his care. He who is greater than the world can desire nothing from the world. There he is free, stable, fitted for the light of immortality. This new power and dignity is a gift from God, and it is accessible to all. "As the sun shines spontaneously, as the day gives light, as the fountain flows, as the shower yields moisture, so does the heavenly spirit infuse itself into us. When the soul in its gaze into heaven has recognized its author, it rises higher than the sun, and far transcends all this earthly power, and begins to be what it believes itself to be."[8] Gold ceilings and mosaic marbles will seem mean to one who knows that it is himself who is to be perfected, is to be adorned, and that the all-important temple is the temple of the soul in which the Holy Spirit has begun to make His abode. All other beauty shall perish but this remains, "perpetual, vivid, in perfect honor, in permanent splendor."[9]

Cyprian's conversion was radical from the start. In this respect it was like that of the early Methodists. He abode in no half-way house, partly Christian, partly pagan. He was now Christ's, and he served Him henceforth according to his light with undeviating loyalty. The Christianity to which he was converted was not entirely that of Paul— 200 years lay between; it was the semi-Scriptural, semi-Catholic Christianity of A. D. 250, various traits of which we shall see as we go forward. But such as it was, Cyprian accepted it with intelligent

---

[8] Ad. Donat. 14 (Ep. 1).   [9] Ibid. 15.

and unselfish devotion from which he never swerved for a moment. To show and test his genuineness this rich rhetorician sold the most of his possessions and gave to the Church for distribution to the poor, sick, and other stricken classes. His house in Carthage, however, was bought back by the Church and given to him again. He entered upon a life of fasting, prayer, and especially of the diligent study of the Holy Scriptures, of which his writings reveal large and exact acquaintance, not neglecting the Church teachers before him, and especially his beloved Tertullian.

The year of his baptism we do not know exactly —probably about 245 or 246. But the day on which the Carthaginian Roman lawyer, Thascius Cyprian, went under what he calls the "birth-giving water" —probably on the beach of his own beautiful bay— was one of the most important days in the history of men. In him the Catholic era became crystallized in forms one sees in almost every church one passes.

CHAPTER III.

CYPRIAN'S JUDGMENT OF HEATHENISM.

It is hardly conceivable that so thoughtful and well-read a man as Cyprian could have had much heart in his paganism. He must have been like many in that Græco-Roman world—externally attached to the faith of the State, but with no love for it, no interior drawing. As soon as he is converted and has to justify his new attitude, he turns against the religious life of heathenism with an earnestness and intelligence and moral revulsion which show that the old religion came to him but found nothing in him.

Like others of the fathers, Cyprian believed the gods were demons who had gotten men in their possession and persuaded them to worship them instead of God. These demons were themselves cast out by Christians, which is a sure proof to him of their frailty and contemptibleness. He challenges the heathen: O, would you but see them and hear them (the demons) when they are adjured by us, and tortured with spiritual scourges, and are ejected from possessed bodies, when, howling and groaning at the voice of man and the power of God, they confess the judgment to come. These demons (gods) are subject to Christians! And yet you worship them. You will see that we are entreated by those whom you entreat, that we are feared by those whom you fear, whom you adore. You will see that under our hands they stand bound and tremble as captives, whom you look up to and venerate as gods. Can you not be convinced as to what kind of gods you worship when you see and hear them upon our interrogation betraying what they are, and even in your presence unable to conceal those deceits and trickeries of theirs?[1]

The casting out of demons was a large function in the early Church. Some have seen in this an evidence of the credulity and childishness of the times. But as to the reality of the phenomena, the reality of the cures, there can be no doubt. The question is as to their interpretation. The true view is that in certain ages of civilization, and in certain stages of moral lapse, evil spirit or spirits really take possession in some sense of the person, and according

---

[1] Ad Demetrianum, 15.

to the laws of the soul work there to his physical, mental, and moral ruin. It is not more irrational to believe in the existence of evil spirits than in that of good spirits, or even that of bad men. And if they exist, it is according to the laws of psychology that they may obtain control of human spirits. What was seen in the early Church is seen to-day in some countries.[2] In this realm of evil possession the Church wrought mighty victories for sanity and morality. But interpreting the demons as heathen gods was another matter.

The author of "Quod idola dii non sint" (That Idols are not Gods), generally attributed to Cyprian, has another philosophy of the gods. He says that the gods were formerly kings, who as soon as they died began to be adored by their people. Hence temples were founded to them, images made to them, sacrifice paid and festal days appointed. So to posterity these rites became sacred which at first had been adopted as a consolation. He proves this by the stories of the works of these gods on earth. Apollo fed the flocks of Admetus, Neptune founded walls for Laomedon, the cave of Jupiter is seen in Crete, and his sepulcher is shown,[3] etc.

---

[2] See the valuable book of Nevius, Demon Possession and Allied Themes, New York, 1894.   [3] Quod Idola, 1, 2.

CYPRIAN'S JUDGMENT OF HEATHENISM.

When it is said that to these gods Rome owes its greatness, the writer replies that that is due simply to the vicissitudes and chances of fortune. But Rome has no real moral greatness, and never had. A lot of criminals and profligates come together, found an asylum, by impunity for crimes made their number great. Romulus himself was a fratricide. When they want marriage they begin that "affair of concord by discords." They steal, they do violence, they deceive,—anything to get people. Their marriage consists of broken covenants of hospitality and cruel wars with their fathers-in-law. Brutus puts his sons to death that the commendation of his dignity may increase by the approval of his wickedness.[4] How did this plain speaking strike the haughty Roman?

But this author gets round to the demon theory. They are impure and wandering spirits, who after having been steeped in worldly vices, lost their celestial vigor by the contagion of earth, and now, ruined themselves, seek to ruin others. Even poets acknowledge the existence of demons, and Socrates said he was instructed by one. From them magi have power for mischief or for mockery, though the chief of them, Hostanes, said that the form of

---
[4] Quod Idola, 5.

the true God can not be seen, and that true angels stand around His throne. Plato believed this also, maintaining one God, the rest angels or demons. Hermes Trismegistus believed, too, in one God incomprehensible, beyond our ken.[5]

As to the moral content of paganism Cyprian did not mince his words. Nor was he haranguing a crowd or advocating a cause before a jury, when he might be tempted, like our political orator, to exaggerate; but he is giving his sober thoughts to a friend who could not be deceived. Both knew their world. Cyprian, at least, we may assume, knew it thoroughly. And he finds nothing to regret for having left it: the roads blocked up with robbers, seas beset with pirates, wars everywhere. The world is wet with mutual blood and murder, which for an individual is called a crime, is called a virtue when it is committed wholesale.[6] Was there ever a finer description of most wars than that? The quickened conscience of the early Christians

---

[5] Quod Idola, 6. Though scholars are now generally agreed that the Quod Idola dii non sint is not the work of Cyprian (see Haussleiter, Cypr. Studien. Comment. Woefflin, Leipz. 1891, 379 ff, Ehrhard, Die altchristliche Literatur und ihre Erforschung, Freib. i. B, 1900, 462), yet it is undeniable that its thought moves in the Cyprianic circle. It is a compilation from Minucius Felix, Tertullian, and Cyprian. As the latter borrowed wholesale from the others, one may fairly take the Quod Idola as representing Cyprian also.

[6] Ad Donatum, 6.

detested war, but they did not detest it more than it deserved.

He then turns his attention to that beloved institution of paganism—the gladiatorial shows. Men who have committed no crime are fattened for this slaughter. "Man is slaughtered that man may be gratified and the skill that is best able to kill is an exercise of an art. Men train to murder. Men of ripe age and beautiful person offer themselves for this horrible combat. Think of it! Fathers look down on their sons; a brother is in the arena and his sister hard by. The increased pomp of the show makes the tickets higher, yet even the mother will pay the increased price to witness her child's death-wound on a gala-day. Yet with all these frightful scenes they are not at all conscious that they are parricides with their eyes."[7] And it needed the introduction of Christianity to distinguish between murder, torture, a thousand deaths and—sport!

As to the theater, though it does not take life like the gladiatorial shows, it kills virtue—and it must be confessed that, though it has changed for the better under Christianity, it is still sufficiently true to its reputation in Cyprian's time. Parricide and incest are unfolded in action, so that as the ages

---

[7] Ad Donatum, 7.

pass, old crimes may not be forgotten. On the stage the old wickedness and impiety still live on. By the teaching of infamies in the mimes the spectator is reminded of what he may have done or may yet do. Adultery is learnt while it is seen; and having public authority this mischief panders to vices and works havoc among modest women. Besides "what a degradation of morals, what a stimulus to abominable deeds, what a food for vice, to be polluted by stage gestures, and against the covenant and law of one's birth to gaze in detail upon incestuous abominations." They show Venus immodest, Mars adulterous, and that Jupiter of theirs not more supreme in dominion than in vice, etc. And now put the question, says Cyprian: Can he who looks upon such things be healthy-minded or modest? Men immitate the god they adore,—their crimes become their religion.[8]

This Zola-like painter of a world he knew so well then refers to that vice[9] which ancient literature reveals as frightfully common,—impossible to believe as our feelings make it. Is it possible that paganism, glorified by our freethinkers, had first to hear from the new despised faith protests against the unnatural diabolical lusts which its best men

---

8 Ad Donatum, 8.   9 Rom. i, 26, 27.

Cyprian's Judgment of Heathenism. 33

looked upon as a matter of course? But in Cyprian's day it would seem that the higher morality of Christianity was bringing some of the guilty to consciousness at least. He speaks of these accusing others in order to escape their own condemnation,—accusers in public criminals in private; people imbruted with the madness of vice deny what they have done, and yet hasten to do.[10]

The sacred seat of law itself is defiled. Wickedness is done in the very face of the statutes, and the Forum echoes with the madness of strife. Then the punishments—the claw that tears, the rack that stretches, the fire that burns—and of these the poor Christians had knowledge. Who is to help? The patron? He deceives. The Judge? He sells his sentence. The very judge becomes the culprit that the innocent may perish. Crimes are everywhere. One man forges a will, another makes a false oath; children are robbed of their inheritances; on all sides the "venal impudence of hired voices falsifies the charges, while the guilty do not even perish with the innocent. There is no fear about the laws; no concern for either inquisitor or judge; when the sentence can be bought off for money, it is not cared for."[11] We often hear about the majesty of Roman

---

[10] Ad Donatum, 9.   [11] Ibid. 10.

law, the respect for justice, and all that, and there was a time and a season in which these things were realities; but the relentless pen of Rome's own lawyers uncovered the rottenness of an age and a civilization which our easy-going pagan idealists hold up for admiration.

In another place, speaking of plagues, Cyprian says that they only give opportunity for avarice and rapine. In these times people do not show affection, but are rash in quest of impious gains. They shun the deaths of the dying, but crave the spoils of the dead, so that it looks as if the wretched were forsaken in their sickness, lest being cared for they might recover. Everywhere there is seizing, everywhere taking possession—no dissimulation about spoiling, no delay. Thieves conceal themselves in ravines and rob under cover of darkness. Avarice rages openly, exposes its weapons in the marketplace. "Thence cheats, thence poisoners, thence assassins in the midst of the city,—these are eager for wickedness as they are wicked with impunity." Judges are for sale. It might appear from such books as Steffens's "Shame of the Cities" (New York, 1904), that corruption could not well be more appalling in the Roman Empire than in some of the cities of our Christian America, and especially in

Philadelphia, which, under the Quay ring and its successor, seems to bear the palm for political and financial and other debauchery. But as a matter of fact, such towns are as the isles of Araby the Blest by the side of conditions revealed to us in both the pagan and Christian literature of ancient times.

CHAPTER IV.

A POPE.

One of the first books written by Cyprian after his conversion was his "Testimonies Against the Jews," though it was not written till he had saturated himself through and through with the Scriptures. His method is simple. After the manner of a lawyer he presents his case in a series of brief numbered propositions, and then takes each thesis in order and proves it simply by quotations from both Old and New Testaments, especially the Old. His book is dedicated to a young Christian friend, Quirinus, to whom he says that if he wants strength and intelligence, he must "examine more fully the Scriptures, old and new, and read through the complete volume of the spiritual books." All patristic literature is evidence of the loyal and hearty attitude of the Christians to the Bible, undeterred by the fear least some would read it too much or be misled by their own interpretations. Cyprian calls the Scriptures the "spring of the divine fullness," and he urges Quirinus "to drink more plentifully and be more abundantly satisfied."[1]

The propositions concerning the Jews which he seeks to prove are such as these: that they have fallen under the wrath of God because they have left Him for idols; because they slew the prophets; that they do not understand their Scriptures and never will until they believe on Christ; that it was foretold that they would lose their land, that their old law would cease, that a new one would come, that a new prophet would arise, that Gentiles would receive the Christ, that they would take the place of the Jews in the Divine favor, but that the Jews can still be saved if they with baptism wash away the blood of Christ slain, and passing over into the Church obey His precepts. These and other propositions are thus proved in order simply by quotations from the Scriptures.

The second book is taken up with propositions concerning Christ, which show that Cyprian would have been a stanch supporter of Athanasius. Christ is the First-born, the Wisdom of God, the Word of God, is God, was incarnated in our race, born of a virgin, Man and God, Son of man and Son of God; that in the passion and sign of the cross is all virtue

---

[1] Test. adv. Jud., Introd.

and power; that it is impossible to attain to God the Father except through Christ the Son, and the latter is to come as Judge, and is to reign as King forever. The last book is a series of miscellaneous propositions in religion and morals proved in the same way. The only apocryphal book quoted is Ecclesiasticus. His use of Scripture is of course entirely arbitrary; and though he often hits upon apposite and telling passages to prove his points, he shows no scientific principles of interpretation, and seizes upon Old Testament passages helter-skelter as though they were all equally literal and equally applicable to the Christian religion and to present circumstances.

A prominent rhetorician, who upon his conversion sold his estate and devoted himself to sacred studies, showed immediately that he was called to the ministry. He was therefore made deacon immediately, in 247 was made presbyter, and in 248 bishop. He went through the two first years so quickly and so soon made a bishop that we have hardly any account of his activity in the last stations. What was a bishop about 250, and how was he elected?

The laity were the commons or plebs, the clergy, the *ordo,* that is, the senatorial order of the Church.[2]

See Benson, 19, who has correctly represented the facts here.

Both had distinctive rights, for both belonged to the flock of Christ. The laity had privileges of which they have long since been robbed by the hierarchical Church. As the senators in court and in basilica had the common bench (consessus), so had the clergy in the congregation. Did this difference between commons (laity) and senators (orders, or clergy) rest upon a divine anointing of the latter which set them apart as *in essence* a separate caste through whom alone the life of God could come to men? Were they the indispensable means of communicating grace on account of a sacred function which they shared among themselves solitary and incommunicable? Or was their place rather that of custom and use, for good order and decency of administration, by the ordinance of the Church, divine (of course) in a sense, but not as excluding laymen from the same grace and functions if necessity should arise? Was the source of their power God acting solely through clerical officers, or God acting through the whole Church?

The "Master" Tertullian did not answer these questions in the present "Catholic" sense. He remained true, at least measurably, to the original democratic and spiritual conception of the Church. "The authority of the Church," he says, "makes the difference between order [*ordinem,* clergy] and people, and honor [or office of the clergy] is consecrated by the common bench of the order. Where there is no common bench [of the clergy] you [laymen] offer [administer the Lord's Supper], you baptize, and you are priest alone for yourself. For where three are the Church is, even if they are laymen."[3] Tertullian is always true to that conception. He does indeed except women from any ministerial function, but that is entirely on account of their sex.[4] He blames the heretics also for inextricably mixing up laity and clergy, and observing no decent order, capriciously "enjoining sacerdotal offices on laymen," but he is here speaking of an apparently reckless disregard of all order.[5] In his work on baptism he also has in mind this observance of decent administration. He says the chief priest, that is, the bishop, has the right of administering baptism if he is present, after him the presbyters and deacons, though not without the bishop's authority, "on account of the honor of the Church, which being preserved peace is preserved. Beside these, laymen have the right, for what is equally received can be equally given. Unless

---

[3] De Exhort. Cast. 7. [4] De Veland. Virg. 9. [5] De Præscrip. Haeret. 41.

A Pope. 41

bishops or priest or deacons be on the spot, other disciples are called to the work." Tertullian lays down the great principle that ought to be dear to every Christian: *The Word of the Lord ought not to be hidden by any,* a principle on which the early Methodists went, by which they won their triumphs. "In like manner, too, baptism, which is equally God's property, may be administered by all."[6] In Tertullian's mind all Christian men are as really priests as the Jewish priests, and so he thought that all Christians, like the Jewish priests, were bound to single marriages only.[7] The Levitical priesthood typified to Tertullian not the sacerdotal *ordo* (clergy), but the universal priesthood of Christians. "In his time," says Benson well, "the substantive priesthood of the laity was an understood reality."[8] He believed of course in the official priesthood of the clergy, and I do not say that he had thought through the doctrine of the ministry according to Christianity. But he came much nearer to it than Cyprian.

In the twenty-five years that had elapsed between the two great Carthaginians, the Catholic tide had not stood still, and Cyprian was farther up the shore than Tertullian. With him the bishop was

---

[6] De Baptismo, 17.   [7] De Monog. 7.   [8] Cyprian, 21.

not simply the representative of the people in their priestly capacity, officially taking up in himself their priestly character. No, he is much greater. He represents not the people but Christ Himself. He is *the priest,* not so much *episcopus* as *sacerdos.* The Jewish priesthood typifies not the Christian nation of priests, but the clergy. The rights and privileges of the old priesthood passed at the crucifixion to the Christian bishop; each congregation is the "congregation of Israel;" the election of a bishop is made in accordance with the law of Moses; the presbyters are the Levites, and when they approach the people are to rise up, as Lev. xix, 32, commands. The bishops are also apostles, they succeed in ordination from the apostles; they stand by divine creation, not by historic or ecclesiastical right alone; the diaconate may be a human institution, but not the bishops. These are also judges. They judge in Christ's stead. To dispute the bishop's decision is to be a heretic. Even to keep the faith and the true worship, and yet invade the office of bishop is the sin of Korah. The Old Testament laws about High Priest apply to bishops alone.[9] "Verily he [the bishop] officiates as a priest in the place of

---

[9] Ep. 8 (2), 1; 67, 1, 4, 9; 65, 2; 3 (64), 3; 66 (68), 4; 59 (54), 5; 66 (68) 3 (64); 59 (54); 43 (39).

Christ, because he imitates what Christ did, and offers the sacrifice true and full [in the Lord's Supper] in the Church to God the Father."[10]

It will not do to say that all this was an air-castle, though it was; so far as resting on any real basis in Scripture or in fact it was as unsubstantial as last year's dreams. But to Cyprian it was the most real thing in the world. And it was sufficiently in accord with the Catholic evolution of the second and third centuries as—when supported by Cyprian's piety, reputation, persistence, and exegesis (arbitrary, fantastic, false though it was)—to make a profound impression, set the results of that evolution in permanent shape, and make his little cycle in that Tunisian city the determining reckoning for all Christians and for all time.

When Cyprian came on the scene, the bishop was the head officer in the local Church, there being a bishop in every town. Against him persecution was directed; the confiscation of his property was sometimes the only edict of the magistrate; he sat in the center of the row of presbyters or on a chair above them; he was the chief preacher; only he administered communion, or in his absence those whom he commissioned; baptism was also mainly

---

[10] Ep. 63 (62), 14.

confined to him; he was judge in disputes and the chief office as to disqualifications for Church functions. Cyprian added nothing to the substance of the bishop's power, he only placed it on a religious basis. He sanctified it with the halo of the Old Testament law.

How was the bishop elected? The laity gave Cyprian to the Church. If the filling the vacancy caused by the death of Donatus had been left to the clergy, we would never have heard of him. The latter thought he was immature in religious experience, a novice, and so, according to Paul (1 Tim. iii, 6), ineligible for Church office. Cyprian thought so himself and declined, wishing an older presbyter to be elected. But the people were inexorable. They looked upon him as the strongest and wisest minister in the city, and they would not be refused. They surrounded his house, filled all approaches, cut off escape, and compelled him to accept. According to Cyprian there were three or four things necessary in every election of bishop: the judgment of God, the voice of the people, the choice of the bishops of the province, and the testimony of the clergy. But what was the relation of each of these elements to the other, the relative importance of each one, and how each was expressed, we do not know. He says it is divine tradition and apostolic observance—it was not, Cyprian had no exact historical knowledge—that "for the proper celebrations of ordinations all the neighboring bishops of the same province shall assemble with that people for which a prelate is ordained. And the bishop shall be chosen in the presence of the people, who have most fully known the life of each one, by the suffrage of the brotherhood and by the sentence of the bishops assembled."[11] He emphasizes the suffrage of the people,[12] and once the testimony of his colleagues.[13] It does not appear that the neighboring bishops gave any formal vote to the election of Cyprian, nor that his co-presbyters did, but that the one decisive factor was the clamant call of the people. In other words he was elected by acclamation of the people, which was confirmed by the later assent of all the presbyters except five, and by the ordination of the bishops. According to Cyprian, the assembled bishops had the right of election, with the co-operation of the clergy; but as Böhringer well says, the election itself depended in the last instance upon the consent or veto of the congregation.[14] The laity had the first and the last and decisive voice, though probably did not vote as in a formal election. In fact, we do not know from Cyprian's Epistles that any one cast a vote. But

[11] Ep. 67, 5.   [12] 59 (54), 5. 6.   [13] 44 (40), 2.

it is striking that the greatest Churchman of the third century was really made a bishop by laymen, that there was still existing by the side of the growing hierarchy this instructive survival of original congregationalism.[15]

Cyprian was the first pope, that is, the first bishop repeatedly called papa, papas, or pope,[16] and that too, on the part of the Roman Church. I do not lay stress on this, but call attention to it as showing that the exclusive use of the word by Rome since the decree of Hildebrand, 1073, and the generally exclusive use since the eighth century, is on par with most of her usurpations. Apparently the first bishop to be so called was Heraclas of Alexandria,[17] who died about 246, the first Roman bishop Marcellinus, 249-304, and in the fourth century bishops of various sees large and small are called pope. If we import the later thought into the word, that is, if we think of the pope as the ruling spirit in the Church, the Roman presbyters are entirely justified in giving the title to him of Carthage, because he and no other was pope in the short but troubled time of his episcopate.[18]

---

[15] For the part of the laity in the election of bishops, as witnessed by Origen, Eusebius, etc., see Haddon, art. Bishop in Dict. Chr. Antiq. i, 214.

[16] Eps. 30; 31 (25); 36 (29); 23 (16); 8 (2); at beginning.

[17] Eus., H. E. 7, 7.

[18] On the title pope see Benson, 29-31. Mullinger, in Dict. Chr. Ant. ii, 1652, 1663-4.

CHAPTER V.

BEFORE THE STORM.

CYPRIAN became bishop probably in July, 248, and the Decian persecution began at the end of 249 or the beginning of 250. The Church had had peace since the death of Sulpicius Severus, February 4, 211—almost forty years. What chance for quiet growth and development, for missionary work, for literary achievements, etc.? But alas! this promise was not kept, or only partially kept. The Church grew, indeed, but at the expense of purity, and there was little of literary work between Tertullian and Cyprian. Then were laid the seeds of the Novatian schism. A time of peace for nation or Church imposes special obligations of watchfulness and discipline and self-denial, lest corruptions creep in and the inheritance be lost. And in a Catholic Church these corruptions are almost inevitable. When sacraments take the place of a transforming faith in a personal Savior, when Church absolution takes the place of divine forgiveness and conversion, when harmony with the bishop is practically substituted for ethical and spiritual harmony of the life with God, union with Christ interpreted in terms of union with the Church, when Christianity is thus externalized and superficialized as it is in the so-called Catholic Churches, a series of miracles is necessary to keep the Church pure. That God will not prevent by extraordinary means what may be avoided by the simple paths of His Gospel, history is a witness. Look at Russia, to-day, whose battleships are furnished with both icons and harlots, or in France where priests and mistresses used to jostle each other in the corridors of the Most Catholic King.

In the eighteen months of Cyprian's episcopate before the outbreak of the persecution, it was his noble aim to purify the Church as well as he could by discipline. "Long peace had corrupted," he said, "a divinely delivered discipline; faith had been taking her ease and was half asleep."[1] First he tried to break up the practice of the clergy assuming worldly responsibility, whether as tutor or in trades or professions. It is well known that for hundreds of years it was not uncommon for ministers to be engaged in secular occupations, like the local preachers of Methodism. "A clergyman, learned

---
[1] De Lapsis, 5.

in the Word of God," says an ancient statute, "May seek support by work as much as he likes;" and again: "A clergyman may satisfy himself with food and clothing by working as an artisan or by agriculture, barring detriment to his office."[2] We read of one who tended sheep, another (a bishop) a weaver, another a shipbuilder, a lawyer, etc.[3] By and by this was practically done away by a salary or regular Church income.[4] During the peace the clergy, including even the bishops, not only worked or traded for a living, but pushed their secular work with vigor for pure gain,—"they with insatiable ardor of covetousness devoted themselves to the increase of their property." The bishops "despised the divine charge, became agents in business, deserted their people, wandered about in foreign provinces, hunted the markets for gainful merchandise, while brethren were starving in the Church. They sought to possess money in hoards, they seized estates by crafty deceits, they increased their gains by multiplying usuries."[5]

A case was presented to Cyprian of one who in

---

[2] Statuta Eccl. Antiqua, cc. 51, 52.
[3] Socrates, H. E. 1, 12; Sozomen, 7, 28; Greg. Mag. Ep. 13, 26; see note 23 in Hatch, Organization, etc., p. 151; Ludlow in Dict. Chr. Ant. I 409-11; Hatch in same, II, 1489-91.
[4] On this see von Schubert's Möller, KG. I, 368-9.
[5] Cypr., De Lapsis, 6.

his will had appointed Faustinus, a presbyter, as executor (*tutor*) or curator of his property. The bishop meets the case with decision. No offering shall be made for the deceased, nor sacrifices celebrated for his repose. The poor fellow must get along as best he can in the other world without the prayers and offerings of the living. Cyprian refers to a rule passed by the bishops excluding ministers from serving as executors (though the Roman law made the filling of such appointments obligatory) so that they "may not be called from their divine administration nor be tied down by worldly anxieties and matters."[6] But this severity, though no doubt effective for a time, did not at all break up the secular work of the clergy. He cites the Levitical tithe, argues at this early stage in his usual hierarchical way—the absolute distinction between secular and sacred, the obligatoriness of the Old Testament law, the minister to do only with the altar,—a conception "altogether in contradiction to the original Christian views and forms of organization."[7]

An interesting question was presented by a letter from a distant town. It appears an actor had been received into the Church, having first, of

---

[6] Ep. 1 (65). For offerings for the dead, already in Tertullian, see De Monog. 10. [7] Böhringer, 816.

Before the Storm. 51

course, given up his profession. But on the ground of necessity of living he had been training boys to the same life. The bishop of the little town where the actor lived wrote Cyprian asking whether this could be allowed. The reply is in the true spirit of Tertullian, and in this case in the true spirit of Christian. He refers to the "disgraceful and infamous practices of the theater, emasculation of boys and men,[8] men putting on women's garments, immodest gestures, and the gratification of the desire by the sins of a corrupted and enervated body." If it is a sin for one to act in the theater, is it not to teach others the same? If he is compelled to this by poverty, let the Church support him frugally, and if the Church is not able, let him come to us. Such was the advice of Cyprian. The Church denied baptism and communion to frequenters of the theater, not to speak of actors, and she did wisely in this, because the theater was not only connected with idolatry, but was an inciter and purveyor to sin and vice in various and influential ways,—it was then and ever has remained the foremost opponent to

---

[8] The late Bishop A. Cleveland Coxe is authority for the statement that in the Sistine Chapel of the Vatican the fine music is obtained by recourse to this expedient inflicted upon children. Note to his edition of Wallis's transl. of Cyprian, p. 356, note 3. See art. Eunuch in Chambers's Encyclopædia ed. 1893 or later. Cyp. Ep. 2 (60).

all the ideals for which the Church stands.[9] Later the Church found she could not carry out such strict laws, as she finds to-day. The theater was too much for her. Then her leaders, like Chrysostom, Cyril, and Salvian, had to content themselves with sharp denunciations of it and warnings against it.

To Christians of to-day, virgins occupying the same house with men, often the same room and even the same bed, could not be understood. But in the early centuries that was a common custom, probably due to the necessity of finding homes for converted girls and women who had been disowned by parents. Then, in the exaltation of Christian enthusiasm, in that prophetic ecstasy which characterized some early Christians, in that exaggerated estimate of virginity which was very early introduced, with the freshness of faith in the power of the new life, there can be no doubt that this relation of dwelling together of men and women pledged to virginity, was often, as Achelis has shown, absolutely innocent of immorality. But as time passed and the old enthusiasm died away, and especially as the persecutions ceased and crowds came into the Church, it is evident that this spiritual bond did not

---

[9] See Bingham, Antiquities, bk. 11, ch. 5, sections 6, 9; bk. 16, ch. 4, section 10; and ch. 11. section 12.

Before the Storm.

always remain spiritual. This was recognized by the Council of Nicea, A. D. 325, which prohibited the practice,[10] as did also that of Carthage of 348.[11] Cyprian had to meet this scandal, as he recognizes it, and he does it in a thorough and straightforward manner. He cuts up the whole custom, root and branch. Virgins must not even live with men in this way, not to speak of anything else. Those who have slept with men must be examined by midwives before they can receive communion again. Purity must be kept at all hazards. Cyprian's letter is a noble plea for discipline. No doubt it had its effect, but the continuance of the practice for centuries shows that the question of the relation of men to women, of both to pledges to virginity, had not been solved by the ancient Catholic Church, which very early adopted a false and unchristian asceticism, and thus helped along the condition referred to as well as the corruption with which monasticism has made us familiar. Perhaps they were too near to the universal pagan customs of bathing and sleeping together. A new civilization had to come.[12]

---

[10] Can. 3. [11] Can. 3, 4.
[12] Cyprian Ep. 4 (61). See also Coxe in Ante Nic. Fathers II, 57–8; Benson, 54 and notes; Venables, in Dict. Chr. Antiq. II, 1939–41; and esp. H. Achelis, Virgines Subintroductæ; ein Beitrag, etc., Leipz. 1902.

Great Christians from Tertullian to Wesley have not considered woman's dress a subject too insignificant for treatment. Cyprian wrote one of his most vigorous treatises on this subject. No doubt he had more provocation than Wesley, for heathen society fostered adornments, luxurious, excessive, unchaste, to which doubtless the eighteenth century at its worst could not approach. But many of Tertullian's and Cyprian's (who borrowed from him wholesale) denunciations are as appropriate to-day as then. Has God willed, asks Cyprian, who as a mere man could not see either the beauty or right of self-mutilations and dyeings and the efforts to improve on God,—has God willed that holes should be made in the ears, by which the children should be put to pain, so that subsequently heavy beads should be hung? Such arts as the sinning and apostate angels put forth. It was they who taught women to pain the eyes around with a black circle, to stain the cheeks with a deceitful red, to change the hair, and drive out truth both of face and head. Then adulterations and various colorings are laying hands on God, whose work is perfect. Cyprian lashes all this artificial making-up with burning words. In fact, for virgins who are given to Christ he repudiates adornments of any kind. Why should she walk out adorned? Why with dressed hair, as if she either had or sought for a husband? Rather let her dread to please, if she is a virgin; let her not invite her own risk if she is keeping herself for better and divine things. These should also keep away from marriage parties, with their lascivious talk, with their disgraceful words and drunken banquets, where the "bride is animated to bear, and the bridegroom to dare lewdness." So also she should flee the baths, where modesty is laid aside, vice is enticed,—these promiscuous baths, "fouler than a theater." Is it any wonder the Church mourns over her virgins; hence she groans over their scandalous and detestable stories; hence the flower of her virgins is extinguished. At the close Cyprian praises virginity, which is free from the sorrows and pains of women, the pangs of child-bearing, the worship of husband, which possesses already the glory of the resurrection, which passing through the world without the contagion of the world is equal to the angels of God.[13]

From these earliest writings of Cyprian we can readily see the conditions of the Christian Church on the eve of the Decian persecution. Some bishops were so engrossed in money-making that they neg-

---

[13] De Hab. Virg. 4, 14, 18, 19, 20, 22.

lected their work, some were even usurers. There was a free-living bishop who made his office a means of gain, ready to abjure the faith on occasion, and ready to take it up again when danger was over. "Cyprian had," says Augustine,[14] "not a private table, but God's altar in common with his colleagues,—usurers, the insidious, cheats, robbers." Some were mixed up with dishonest practices in fairs and others in the slave trade of the Sahara. "Some were too ignorant to prepare their catechumens for baptism, or to avoid heretical phrases in their public prayers," and too ignorant or too careless not to use in their liturgies the compositions of well-known heretics. Among the clergy there were makers of idols and compounders of incense, and among the laity astrologers and theatrical trainers.[15]

Not a moment too soon did Cyprian come on the scene. His remedy was "discipline,—discipline the safeguard of hope, the bond of faith, the guide of the way of salvation, the stimulus and nourishment of good dispositions, the teacher of virtue, which causes us to abide always in Christ, and to live continually for God, and to attain the heavenly promises and the divine rewards."[16] The remedy

---

[14] Aug. De Bap. c. Donat. VII, 45 (89).
[15] Tertullian, De Idolatr. 7, 9; Cyp. Ep. 2 (60). [16] De Hab. Virg. 1.

was good, and woe to the Church where discipline is a lost art. But the disease was deep, and Cyprian's remedy touched the surface only. What was needed was a true Christianity. That was then historically impossible, but a storm was at the doors which did the work in another fashion.

CHAPTER VI.

THE DECIAN PERSECUTION.

Why did Rome persecute the Christians? That is a question whose answer at first seems easy, but the more one studies it the more difficult it becomes. The law of the Twelve Tables forbade strictly anyone to worship strange gods unless they were adopted by the State. But what would be done when foreign lands were conquered? Would their gods be virtually adopted by Rome, who took in, as a matter of fact, the whole Greek pantheon? Now as it never was an offense for the native to worship his native gods, it is evident that Rome either winked at these strange cults or in effect adopted them as her own. The former was the fact. The Isis worshiper had long been domiciled in the capital, and, excepting the bloody Druid religion of Gaul, Rome never interfered in the slightest with the aboriginal faith of her conquered lands. But what was the matter with Christianity that it could not share a like toleration? Chiefly this, that it claimed to be a monotheistic religion, the only true, absolute religion, and a missionary religion too, destined for universal conquest, whom every man must receive to be saved. Well, what of it? Why could not Rome stand that? Because her own religion was identified with the State, glorified and made divine by the State, which in its turn it glorified and made divine. It was the State in its godward or religious aspect. The State found its head, its incarnation, in the emperor, who thus became himself divine. Now the polytheistic religions found no fault in this. Each one was a State religion, and they did not stumble in acknowledging the supreme Roman religion over all. For this reason the boasted tolerance of Rome stopped at Christianity. As a great Church historian says, the "tolerance of the State had polytheism as a presupposition."[1] But Judaism was monotheistic, and that was tolerated. Yes, but Judaism was a national faith which did not try to make proselytes, and which as to its chief center of worship had ceased to exist after A. D. 70. It did not present at all the same problem to the State as Christianity.

It is true that popular clamor imputed fearful

---

[1] Von Schubert's Möller, Kirchengeschichte, I, 181 (1902). So also Harnack in the Hauck-Herzog. 3 Aufl. III, 827-8 (1897).

crimes to the Christians,—murder, incest, child-eating, and abominable deeds of darkness, and it may be there were cases in which the adverse decision of the magistrate was determined by these alleged crimes. But it is a fact that they play no part— or at least a very small part—in our historical sources. Almost always the action turns on the charge of sacrilege and treason (*lèse majesté*), and the former because of the latter. The accused is asked to sacrifice to the gods or to the emperor's image,—one or both, and it made no difference which. If he refused the former, he was guilty of sacrilege (*sacrilegium*), if the latter, *majestas* or treason, but every time the former had fatal consequences only because it implied in the mind of the pagan Roman the latter. As a mere religion Christianity might have been tolerated. Most of its religious peculiarities were a matter of indifference to the authorities, and its moral teachings often commended it to them. It was only when the political side of its monotheism came out that the sword fell. When Tertullian in his powerful *Apology* speaks of the Roman religion as a religion, he treats it with jokes, scorn and derision: he knew he could do that. But when he comes to the political side of it in its bearing upon the Christians he labors hard and soberly to show that the political side receives no injury, that the Christians are loyal and reverent to the emperor. Though they will not offer to him, they pray for him, and are absolutely faithful to him in every political relation.

It must be remembered that until Decius there were no express laws against the Christians as such. Their trials proceeded always under the general police or criminal jurisprudence of the empire; which was not closely defined or limited, but was general and elastic, and left large play to the individual judgment or caprice of the president of the court who was the prefect, proconsul, or governor. The civil law of Rome was fixed fast, with well understood rules; the criminal law was not. It was something like the police power of a modern State, which can soon override the people's liberties in case of assumed necessity, like an uproar, mutiny, riot, etc., or like the power of a ship captain. For this reason a tolerant and free thinking governor, or even a careless and Gallio-like one, could let the Christians go if he thought there were no immediate danger to the State; while an upright and strict ruler, patriotic and devoted to the national ideals, could easily set the forces of persecution at work. Strictly speaking, as Harnack says, there were no persecutions (except perhaps that of Nero) in ancient times. They were always covered by the general law of police—a nation's law of self-preservation. But emperors and governors would interpret and apply the law according to their character or disposition, or according to circumstances, the local situation, etc. Popular clamor, too, played a far larger part than it ought in both pagan and Christian Rome's persecutions, as it plays to-day in lynch-law and other outbreaks in the United States. At any rate, all can understand from this why persecutions were sporadic and intermittent, why there were long stretches of time with comparative peace, when the Church therefore grew with leaps and bounds. Probably there was not a decade, perhaps not a year, without its persecutions; still up to the time of Decius no general or far-reaching measures of repression were undertaken. Origen says that only a few suffered for the Christian cause.[2] "In increasing measure," says Harnack, "Christians were in all conditions in life and in all professions,

---

[2] He was writing about 245, and his words are: "For in order to remind others that by seeing a few engaged in the struggle for their religion they also might be better fitted to despise death, some on special occasions, and these individuals, which could be easily numbered, endured death for the sake of Christianity,—God not permitting the whole nation to be exterminated, but desiring that it should continue, and that the whole world should be filled with this salutary and religious doctrine,"—Contra. Cels. 3, 8.

whose Christian position was notorious[3] without a hair of their head being crumpled; on the other hand, at times, in some provinces (at the discretion of the governor), and under some emperors, they had to suffer severely."[4]

The Samson athlete, Emperor Maximin the Thracian (235-8), was the first to issue an edict which had for its object the total destruction of the Church as an organization by the destruction of its officers. Happily his edict was still-born. It was left to Decius (249-51) to break the long peace, and to inaugurate the most widespread and relentless persecution which had been known up to his time. I should have said that in these trials for sacrilege and (religious) treason, not only did the president wait for some popular impulse or clamor or appearance of sedition, and, after Trajan, uniformly demand specific charges, though he could go on his own initiative if he wished, in the trials themselves much was also left to the discretion of the court. There were no binding forms in this police court, no universally recognized precedents. The trial might not take over five minutes,—apparently the last hearing of Cyprian did not. Are you a Christian? Yes. Will you offer to the gods

---

[3] Ter., Ap. 1, 42. [4] Hauck-Herzog, 3. Aufl. III, 829.

and to the emperor? No. Let him be punished. Sometimes other forms were used. Almost always the accused could immediately vindicate his loyalty by then and there offering to the gods and to the emperor's image, or by swearing by the genius of the emperor. When he did he was immediately set free, though even this was in part at the discretion of the court. He could be examined by torture, and in the Decian outbreak that horrible method both of securing evidence and of punishing was frequently used. As to punishment, if found guilty, much was also left free. Death was the normal, by beheading, by crucifixion, by being thrown to wild beasts, by starving and other prison tortures. The Roman citizen gained no advantage in trials for sacrilege and *majestas;* if guilty he could be burned or tortured to death as quickly as a barbarian, though the judge might respect his rank and citizenship and order beheading. But here again the president was free. He was not absolutely compelled to sentence to death, he could imprison, or banish, or sentence to the mines (generally the Sardinian mines, and a fearful punishment). He could, and often did, exhort to penitence, defer the trial, and by various means, fair and foul, induce recantation. Strange uncertainties

THE DECIAN PERSECUTION.

hung around these Roman criminal-police trials. Did these uncertainties make the Christian's lot lighter or harder? As to maidens or women, it was wild beasts, burning, imprisonment, banishment, or often houses of ill-fame.

Decius was born near Sirmium from a Roman or Romanized family, was governor of Dacia and Moesia under Philip the Arabian, was commissioned against the Goths, called to the empire by his troops, and defeated and slew Philip, his predecessor, at Verona, 249. What led him to come out against the Christians is not clear. From hints here and there we gather that wrath and jealousy filled him because the national worship was being pushed in the background by the new faith,[5] for which he must therefore have had a genuine regard. He would rather have seen a rival prince than a priest of God established in Rome.[6] He was especially furious against the priests, says Cyprian (tyrannus infestus sacerdotibus), and Gregory of Nyssa adds that he tried to break up the whole organization of the Church.[7] From this it appears that the growth of Church government in a Catholic direction, a growth which had been stimulated so greatly by

---

[5] Greg. Nyss. De Vita Greg. Thaum., Migne (Greek) 46, 944.
[6] Cypr. Ep. 55 (51), 9.   [7] Greg. Nyss. Ibid. 946.

the heresies of the second century, which had now reached a climax in the close world-wide network of deacons, priests, and bishops, and which even now gave to the bishop in Rome a moral supremacy, though more in high-sounding words than in substance, this spiritual kingdom which stood over against the empire, aggressive, infectious, penetrating, a State within a State—it was this organization which excited the jealousy and fear of the emperor and his censor Valerian, his adviser and right hand man, and finally his successor on the throne and on the track of the Christians. Besides he looked upon the clergy as in a sense partisans of his murdered predecessor, Philip the Arabian. Then the millennial anniversary of the founding of Rome, celebrated by that emperor with pomp and games, April 21, 248, served to deepen and clarify the national consciousness, and to sharpen it against those who could not join in the festivities with any heart.[8]

The policy of opportunism which had ruled from Trajan (98ff) to himself was brushed aside. The first determined, systematic, and general measures against the Christians were set on foot in the epoch-making edict of 250. Its wording is lost, but its

---

[8] On these millennial celebrations see Gibbon, Ch. VII, Ed. Smith, I, 459-60.

purport is all too well known. All Christians, without regard to age and sex, shall be asked to sacrifice and to take part in the sacrificial meal; torture shall be used if necessary; if the Christians deny the faith the matter is left to the discretion of the judge; but it is not left to his discretion whether he shall carry out the decree, for that is secured by threats of punishment, and withal by a special sacrificial commission.[9] Sometimes those who confessed were sent away to immediate death by crucifixion, fire, beheading, stoning, or hunger; at other times they were labored with or imprisoned, hoping for recantation. In prison it was expected to break them down by hunger, thirst, heat, or other tortures, so as to save them at last. Celerinus at Rome was even personally besought by either Decius or Valerian to abandon his faith, but without success. "He lay in punishments, but the stronger for them; imprisoned, but greater than those who imprisoned him; lying prostrate, but loftier than those who stood; bound, but firmer than the chains; judged, but more sublime than those who judged him," etc.[10] Among the bishops slain was Fabian in Rome, Alexander in Jerusalem, Babylas in Antioch; while others saved

---

[9] Cypr. Ep. 43 (39): "Five leaders lately associated with a magistrate in an edict." See also the libelli quoted below.   [10] Ep. 39 (33), 2.

themselves by flight, as Cyprian in Carthage, Dionysius in Alexandria, Chæremon of Nilus, and Gregory the Wonder Worker in Neo Cæsarea. The goods of the fled were confiscated, and many of the fugitives were destroyed by the sufferings of the way.

It is unnecessary to say that, with a spiritual condition of the Church such as I have already described, thousands fell away. Would more stand to-day? The majority of the congregation in Carthage immediately disowned Christianity. They could not quickly enough crowd around the officers and get certificates of quittance.[11] When the magistrates wanted to put off the examinations with the coming on of evening, the Christians could hardly submit to the delay. Cyprian scorches them with burning words for this unseemly haste spiritually to destroy themselves. "Why bring with you, O wretched man, a sacrifice? Why immolate a victim? You yourself have come to the altar an offering, you yourself have come a victim; there you have immolated upon salvation your hope; there you have burnt up your faith in the deadly fires."[12] It was the same in other cities, though in Rome more stood firm. "The Church in Rome stands

---

[11] Cyp. de Lapsis, 7.   [12] Ibid. 8.

The Decian Persecution.

firmly in faith, though some have been driven by terror."[13] It was a universal picture of devastation—"look upon the world devastated, and thrown everywhere are the relics and ruins of the fallen."[14] Cyprian sees himself placed "among the ruins of the wailing, the relics of the fearing, the great slaughter of the yielding, and the little firmness of those standing."[15] It was a world-wide sorrow. The confessors felt themselves "placed among various and manifold griefs, on account of the present desolations of many brethren throughout almost the whole world."[16]

Perhaps worse than straightforward denial was the bribery of corrupt officials to place the names of the bribe-givers on the list of the offering ones (*acta facientes*), generally by the presentation of an officially certified paper that such an one had sacrificed (*libellatici*), by which personal appearance before the authorities was avoided. Cyprian says these must repent exactly the same as though they had sacrificed,[17] though he describes some of them as not going to the heathen altars through conscientious motives, and as sending a friend to the officers with the frank avowal that they are Christians and can not come to the demons' "altars,"

---

[13] Cyp. Ep. 8 (2), 2.   [14] Ibid. 30, 5.   [15] Ibid. 11 (7), 8.
[16] Ibid. 31 (25), 1.   [17] De Lapsis, 27.

and that therefore they "pay a price for not doing what is not lawful for me to do."[18] This shows the easy corruptibility of the pagan officers, who almost tempted the Christians to buy their lives ("when the opportunity of securing a certificate was offered"). Let it be said to Cyprian's credit that his ethical sense here was perfectly sound.[19]

Who would have believed that after centuries and more there would have been unearthed these very tell-tale certificates? Did those poor Christians who thus, moved by mortal fear, purchased their safety ever think that their falseness would come forth in the far-off years and condemn them out of the very sands? An interesting illustration of the solemn word, "There is nothing hid that shall not be revealed."[20] In 1893 and 1894 two of these testimonials were dug up in the province of Faioum, southwest of Cairo. One is in the Breugsch collection of the Berlin Museum, the other in that of Archduke Rainer in Vienna. They are little pieces of papyrus leaf, written in Greek, much damaged after their long waiting for the light. They have been skillfully integrated and deciphered, one (the Brugsch) by Dr. Fritz Krebs, the other by Professor K. Wessely. The Rainer papyrus is ac-

---
[18] Ep. 55 (51), 14.   [19] Ep. 30, 3.
[20] Matt. x, 26; Mark iv, 22; Luke xii, 2.

THE DECIAN PERSECUTION. 71

cessible to our readers in the Hurst "History of the Christian Church," I, 243, and I copy here a translation of the Krebs:

"To the commissioners of sacrifice of the village of Alexander's island from Aurelius Diogenes (son of) Satabus, of the village of Alexander's Island. About 72. Scar on right eyebrow. I was both constant in ever sacrificing to the gods, and now in your presence, according to the precepts, I sacrificed and drank and tasted of the victims, and I beseech you to certify this. May you ever prosper. I, Aurelius Diogenes have delivered this." (Then follows in another handwriting, hardly readable, the certificate of the officers) "I Aurelius...... (? saw) him sacrificing. I, Nys (thes, son of).... non have signed.

"First year of the Emperor Cæsar.
    Gaius Messius Quintus
    Trajanus Decius Pius
    Felix Augustus.
2d day of Epiphi.[21] (June 26, 250.)

---

[21] For the Brugsch papyrus see Krebs in Sitzungsberichte d. König. Preus. Akademie d. Wissenschaften zu Berlin, 30. Nov. 1893 (47, 100); Harnack in Theol. Litz. 20. Jan. 1894, 38-41; Kruger, Die neuen Funde auf dem Gebiete der ältesten Kirchengeschichte (1889-1898), Giesen 1898, 17, 18; J. Wordsworth in The Guardian, Jan. 31, 1894, 167. For the Rainer see Wessely in Sitzungsb. d. K. Akad. Wissensch., Phil. Hist. Classe, 141-B Wien. 1894; Harnack in Theol. Litz. 17. März, 1894, 162-3; A. J. Mason in Guardian, March 21, 1894, 431. For both see Appendix B. in Benson, Cyprian 541-4.

But there were thousands of brave ones who would not deny their Lord. The Martyr Acts give us accounts of Pionius and his companions in Smyrna, of Maximus, of Lucianus, and Marcianus, and other names are in the letter of Dionysius to Eusebius[22] and in the letters of Cyprian. The prisons were full of sufferers, and many, especially the clergy, were put to death. We must never think, however, of the wholesale executions—not to speak of massacres—which characterized the Roman Catholic suppression of the Protestants. Nothing like the rescript of Trajan is known in these later annals, and the methodical and carefully legal, though relentless, forms of Decius and Galerius would have seemed almost like Paradise to those who suffered in the wholesale butcheries of the sixteenth century. And to the poor Jews of the Middle Ages, the worst Roman emperor by the side of their Christian persecutors shone white and fair.

We need not be surprised if the devastating effects of the Decian onslaught made a profound impression on the imagination of the Church. It reminded Dionysius of Alexander of the last times before the coming of the Lord;[23] Lucian calls De-

---

[22] Eus. H. E. 6, 40–42. For the martyrologies see Ruinart and the selections of von Gebhardt, 1902, and Preuschen, 1905.

[23] Eus. 6, 41, 10.

THE DECIAN PERSECUTION.

cius the "pioneer of antichrist;"[24] Hilary of Poitiers places his persecution together with that of Nero;[25] Optatus of Mileve thinks of the four beasts of Daniel, and says: "The first beast was as a lion: this was the persecution under Decius and Valerian;"[26] but the worst was the judgment of Lactantius— "the execrable animal Decius."[27]

Professor Victor Schultze makes the point that this persecution can not strictly be called a general one, even if it was so intended. The imperial order was not caried out in some places, and in others only apparently. It was chiefly confined to the cities, though not altogether, as the libelli just referred to show. "The unquiet political relations did not allow systematic measures strongly and consistently to be carried through, and these measures therefore never went farther than having the effect of a quickly passing convulsion."[28]

---

[24] In Cyp. Ep. 22 (21), 1: metator antichristi. Metator is a land measurer, and sometimes the surveyor who goes before to measure land for the camp. [25] Contra Constantium, 4. [26] De Schism. Don. 3, 8. [27] De Mort. Persec, 4. [28] Art. Decius in Hauck-Herzog, 3. Aufl. IV, 528.

CHAPTER VII.

A NEW QUESTION IN DISCIPLINE.

When the storm burst Cyprian secured himself by flight. The heathens of the city cried out violently in the circus and on the streets, "Cyprian to the lions!" His presence in the city made the storm heavier for the Christians, and to relieve them, to save himself for the congregation at a difficult time when they specially needed his guiding and controlling hand, he obeyed the Lord's command,[1] and fled for refuge elsewhere. His hiding place was a secret to the authorities, though known to faithful friends, through whom by letters Cyprian exercised a careful and conscientious oversight over his flock. However little we can blame him, his flight gave to the five dissatisfied presbyters a handle for criticism. They accused him of cowardice and abandoning his flock, and what was specially odious, they wrote to other Churches, especially to Rome, and placed his flight in the worst light. Rome had

---

[1] Matt. x, 23; cf. John xviii, 8.

A NEW QUESTION IN DISCIPLINE. 75

lost her own bishop by martyrdom, and doubtless there were some there who would wonder at this apparent lack of fidelity. They therefore wrote him a letter, which did contain indirect and yet not indistinct reflections.[2] Cyprian defended himself in a letter to his clergy and later to Cornelius in Rome, showed the motive which led him to flee, and besides that already mentioned, referred to visions and Divine commands.

A new question now arose—that is, what is to be done with apostates who desire to return to the Church? This, of course, was not absolutely a new question, because in every persecution there had been such cases. But in the thirty-eight years of peace a new generation had come on the scene. Besides never before had the Church been struck so hard, so suddenly and so universally, and there were crowds of lapsed in nearly every large town. When the persecution ceased after eighteen months, and even before it ceased, many of the unfaithful ones desired to be taken back. With thousands clamoring for admission, the question was by no means so easy as when the Church had only to impose penance on a few. Still more, the question was complicated by martyr certificates, of which later.

---
[2] Ep. 8 (2).

What would the apostolic Church have done with one who in storm of persecution had gone back to heathenism, and later desired to return? After penitence, he would have been received back into full membership. By and by there grew up an artificial distinction in regard to both virtue and sin, at which perhaps asceticism lay at the root. Instead of a heart converted to God and serving Him gladly in the joy of a new life, the Catholic conception of morality grew up which looked upon perfection as the rare attainment of few, notably the abstinent. Then certain sins came to be regarded as so heinous that when once a Christian had committed them, though penitence was required and final salvation not denied, yet the Church herself would not receive the sinner into her ranks again. By the end of the second century this appears to have been the rule. Already in Hermas, about 150, the adulterer can only be received back after the first offense. The second cuts him off finally.[3] Besides, Christ is coming soon, and he will decide the matter Himself.

With the exaggerated emphasis on baptism, due also to the Catholic evolution, it came to be con-

---

[3] Mand. 4: 1, 8. For cropping out of Catholic ideas, see Did. 6, Anc. Hom. (="2 Clem") 7, 3, Herm. Sim. 5, 3.

sidered that while baptism wiped away effectually all former scores, grave sins committed after baptism could find no formal forgiveness here, though the Church would still pray for the offender and hope for the best from God.[4] This conception was all the harder, as Moeller well says, for with the consolidation of the societies into the Catholic Church, which was going on in the latter part of the second century and all through the third, exclusion from one society meant exclusion from the whole Church.[5] The three sins which fell into the category of mortal irremissible sins were murder, adultery, and apostasy to heathenism, and perhaps sins nearly related to them. As early as 177, at Lyons and Vienne in France, it would appear that the guilt of apostasy could be wiped out only by a manful confession at the same or a subsequent persecution,[6] though at Corinth at the same time apparently all sinners could be restored.[7] At about 200 there was a regular scale for penance and punishments; the lighter was confession of ordinary sins and the daily prayer for forgiveness, with warning and correction; the heavier involved exclusion, followed with severe confessions and pen-

---

[4] Iren. 4: 27, 2; Ter., De Pud. 7.   [5] Von Schubert-Möller, KG. I, 279.   [6] Eus. 5: 1, 33, 46.   [7] Ibid. 4: 23, 6.

ances, but ending in return to Church fellowship; the heaviest of all (for the three deadly sins mentioned above) was exclusion from the Church for all time, the offender being placed in the ranks of lifelong penitents and the final decision being referred to God.

Along with this there came the idea of merit, that pardon might be more readily received by ascetic virtues, and that these might compensate for the graver sins and their eternal punishment.[8] So sprung up the idea of satisfaction, which hoped from fasting, kneeling, wearing sackcloth and ashes, etc., to receive special grace and favor,[9] whereas at the beginning the self-denials served only to prove the earnestness of the penitent. The two great Roman jurists, Tertullian and Cyprian, helped to bring in this legal idea,—an externalization of the relations between man and God which has ruled Latin theology from that day to this. If therefore the sinner could in some way get these penitential works to his credit, the way would be opened for his readmittance, even if he were a mortal sinner.

I said a moment ago that the case was complicated in Carthage by the letters of the martyrs. These were simply certificates or briefs issued by

---

[8] Ter. De Poen. 9.   [9] De Poen. 9; De Pud. 5; De Pat. 13.

confessors and martyrs to the effect that the person receiving the letter had done penance for his apostasy from Christianity, and praying or demanding that he be taken in again. The lapsed thronged around the cells of the sufferers, and by importunity, flatteries, weeping, etc., obtains from them those letters of peace, or martyr's certificates of favor. But why did they go to these? Here again we must go back a little. At the beginning the congregation received the penitent acting through the president or elders.[10] But the apostles and prophets, as special bearers of the Spirit, were always looked upon as competent to represent the society in these or other functions, and if any precedence was granted, it was these and not the elders or bishops who enjoyed it.[11] Now after these charismatic offices of apostles and prophets had vanished, martyrs or confessors came to be regarded as having authority something similar, inasmuch as they had stood the highest test of Christianity in the face of threatened death, and thus proved that the power of the Spirit specially dwelt in them.[12] They therefore could forgive sins or mediate the forgiveness of the society. Inasmuch as martyrdom itself

---

[10] Ter. Ap. 39.   [11] 1 Cor. v, 3, 4.   Did. 10, 7.
[12] Hip. De Christ. et Antichrist. 59; Hermas, Vis. 3, 5.

wiped away the stains of the worst sins,[13] it created merit in overabundance, from which it could be communicated to the needy.[14]

One can readily see, therefore, how the martyrs' letters of peace came to play such a large part in the Decian persecution, and how there might arise a jealousy on the part of the bishops in regard to the too zealous exercise of their prerogatives. Little by little, but with the relentlessness of an oncoming tide, the standing office, especially that of bishop, replaced the free charismatic office of apostle and prophet. By the time the second century had passed this substitution was well-nigh complete. By the bishop's mouth the society proclaimed to the sinner forgiveness or excommunication. He had taken into his hands the watching over both doctrine and life. He forgave the lighter sins; he was, in fact, the doorkeeper of the Church.[15] At the bottom Tertullian always looked upon the society itself as proper possessor of the power of the keys,[16] but with that the bishops, as the successors of the apostles, were generally thought of as those who had the right of holding and loosing sins. As a matter of course, the more the official importance of the bishop, the objective worth of his office as mediat-

---

[13] Ter., De Pud. 22.   [14] Eus. H. E. 5: 2, 6, 7.
[15] Ter., De Pud. 14, 18.   [16] Ibid. 21.

ing salvation, waxed, the more his real importance as a man representing the holiness of the Gospel, his subjective character of moral purity, waned. Office took the place of character. "The bishops' office was the natural ally of lax penitential discipline."[17]

It is interesting to see the mixing of these two streams in Tertullian. He considered everything a heavy sin which carries with it an injury of the congregation as the temple of God,[18] and he appropriates the utterance of the Paraclete that the Church has a right to forgive sins because she has the Spirit in her prophets, though from pedagogic motives, she actually does not do it.[19] Idolatry, adultery, and murder are unforgivable sins, so far as Churchly recognition is concerned.[20] The bishop as the organ of the society has the right to forgive lighter sins (delicta leviora), that is, those which do not belong to the three major.[21]

A new stage enters with Callistus, bishop of Rome, who in 217-8 peremptorally issued an edict in which on his own motion he said: "To those who have done penance I remit the sins of adultery and fornication."[22] This novel decree was all the more

---
[17] Von Schubert-Möller, I, 282. [18] De Pud. 19. Cf. the 7 capital sins in Adv. Marc. 4, 9. [19] De Pud. 21. [20] Ibid. 1, 4. [21] Ibid. 18. [22] Ibid. 1.

offensive on account of the history of the man who gave it,—a slave and runaway defrauder, deported to the Sardinian mines for his crimes.[23] In this decree, while admitting that the rights of the congregation and of the martyrs must be preserved, Callistus says that the bishop is the only possessor of the power of the keys in virtue of his apostolic succession. This leads Tertullian to scorn with cutting words the assumption of the "apostolicus," and to reply that as little as the bishops have prophecy and miraculous power, so little have they power of binding and loosing, but rather the prophets.[24] This union of hierarchical claims with loose discipline brought in by the former scoundrel and thief, Bishop Callistus, of Rome, set the pace for Roman Catholic history. It was a principle of Callistus that no bishop could be deposed even for mortal sin, and that the Church must necessarily be composed of sinners, as the tares grew with the wheat.[25] This meant in fact a complete transformation of the idea of the Church. In place of the apostolic thought of the Church as a body of holy people, "called to be saints," the Church became an institution of salvation, in which by an objective holy office the work

---

[23] Hip. Ref. 9, 12.   [24] That is, the Motanist prophets, De Pud. 21. The Montanists kept up the old institution of the prophets, which the general Church had allowed to lapse.   [25] Hip. Ref. 9, 12.

A New Question in Discipline. 83

of instruction is carried on for the sinful members of the society. "The Church is"—not the saints, the believing members of Christ—but, "the number of the bishops."[26] With this elevation of the bishops as the teachers and leaders of the societies, comes also with Callistus the first use of Matt. xvi, 18, as the exclusive property of the Roman see. So his peremptory decision is the preparation for the Roman primacy, and as von Schubert well says, the scornful pleasantries of Tertullian when he derides his brother at Rome,—"pontifex maximus is the bishop of bishops"[27]—is a "prophecy of the future."

---

[26] See Tertullian, De Pud. 21; von Schubert-Möller, I, 284.
[27] De Pud. 1.

CHAPTER VIII.

CYPRIAN, THE LAPSED, AND THE CHURCH IN CARTHAGE.

THE treatment of apostates to heathenism at Carthage is one of the most difficult questions in Church history. It has to be worked out with infinite patience from the Epistles of Cyprian, and to arrange these epistles in order of time is itself a perplexing problem. Thanks to Cyprian experts like Fechtrup, Otto Ritschl, Benson, and Karl Müller, we have now a light and broad path through this thorny thicket. In this chapter I shall follow the guide of Professor Karl Müller, formerly of Breslau, now of Tübingen, who, I think, gives the clearest and most satisfactory statement.[1]

First, as to terms used. Those who were imprisoned or banished for their faith were called confessors by Cyprian. When tortures were used,

---

[1] "Die Bussinstitution in Karthago unter Cyprian," in Zeitschrift für Kirchengeschichte, XVI, 1-44, 187-219 (1895).

CYPRIAN, THE LAPSED.

which was frequently done, especially the laceration of the iron claw, under which death sometimes came as a welcome relief, the sufferers were called martyrs, a term which was also used of confessors who die for any reason. Later Cyprian employed the same word to designate those banished to the mines, but under the expectation of their death.

Now what was the cause of the trouble between Cyprian and some in his Church? The ordinary treatment of the lapsed, as we saw in the last chapter, was simple exclusion—not from the prayers and sympathies of the Church, but from readmittance. But a new element came in when the martyrs and even confessors gave to the deniers of Christ libelli, or letters of peace, testifying to their penitence, forgiving their sins in effect if not in form, and petitioning for their admission. It is unfortunate that the papyrus hunters have not dug up a libellus of this kind, so that we do not know exactly their tenor. On account of the relation of the martyrs to the Spirit referred to before,[2] it was understood that they could give these letters of forgiveness, and that such letters would be favorably considered. But not only did those expecting death give the letters,

---

[2] "Die Bussinstitution in Karthago unter Cyprian," in Zeitschrift für Kirchengeschichte, XVI, 1-44, 187-219 (1895.)

but non-tortured confessors who did not expect death. Later the confessors united and gave letters to all the fallen, to go into effect in case they (the confessors) died. If they did not die, the lapsed invoked the general grant of peace given in the name of the martyr Paulus. This right of the martyrs to forgive mortal sin was a survival of the old power of the prophets, and excited no special comment,—not at least till Callistus struck at the martyrs in favor of the bishops, so that the custom soon came to be for readmission to be carried out by the bishops and congregation alone, though in Carthage still with the co-operation of martyrs.

Cyprian's legal training and conservative spirit made him cling to the martyr's prerogative. No lapsed shall be taken in again who is not supported by the intercession of martyrs. And after he had determined, according to the example of Rome, whose decision ordinarily had great weight with him, that mortal sinners could be received again, he made the condition that they must show a martyr's letter. But this at first only had reference to those lapsed who were sick unto death. For the others Cyprian said that they must wait until the bishops were back from their hiding places and could hold a council in safety, when they would decide what

Cyprian, the Lapsed. 87

weight would be accorded to the martyrs' and confessors' letters to the general run of the lapsed.

In this the martyrs agreed. It does not appear (contrary to Ritschl) that Cyprian and the martyrs were fundamentally at variance, or that the latter expected letters to be *immediately* acted upon; but rather that they should wait till the persecution was over, the lapsed assembled, and investigation made into each case. The old Callistian emphasis on the bishop was thus completely at home in Carthage. What Cyprian is anxious for is not that the martyrs should not have all their rights, but that moral discipline should be guarded. When the confessors communicate to Cyprian (Ep. 23 [16]) that they have granted peace to all the lapsed, he does not see in that a slap at himself, but he fears a despising of his exhortations to moderation in regard to libelli and of evangelical principle in regard to discipline. Lucian, the principal confessor, does not know the Holy Scriptures (Ep. 27 [22]),—right principles as to discipline. The thing will cause hate and difficulties among the lapsed, and the bishop's strictures and reserve will be seen in bad contrast to the large-heartedness of the confessors. It is only the *universality* with which peace is there given which appears to Cyprian the danger:

it threatens to tear discipline to pieces and endangers the bishop's moral position. The Confessors do not threaten in Ep. 23 (16) to withdraw communion from Cyprian, nor do they understand anything more than that the bishops must act on their pardons after sufficient penance on the part of the lapsed, and that these pardons can come into force only at the end of the persecution. Nor do they blame him for his flight.[3] The confessors had never taken up churchly communion with the fallen, to whom they had granted peace. The bishops must first speak, then comes peace.

Now what was the attitude of the presbyters in Carthage to this question? Without waiting for the decision of the bishops, these, on the strength of the peace letters of the martyrs, opened communion immediately with the lapsed.[4] Was this due to the letter of the Roman presbyters to their Carthaginian colleagues,[5] as Ritschl and Harnack think? No. The old view is not well founded that a sharp opposition existed between the presbyters as a whole and their bishop. What happened was that four presbyters[6] wrote to Cyprian in the first stage of the persecution (between February and April, 250) to

---

[3] See Eps. 26 (17) and 27 (22) for Cyprian's reply.
[4] Ep. 15 (10), 1; 16 (9): 2, 3; 17 (11), 2.   [5] Ep. 8 (2).
[6] Donatus, Fortunatus, Novatus, and Gordius.

CYPRIAN, THE LAPSED.

move him to show mildness to the fallen, and to give peace anyhow to the dying. Cyprian did not comply.[7] Soon after came the second stage of the persecution when there was a possibility to help the fallen by the martyrs. Now a part of the presbyters take advantage of this, and on their own motion grant Church communion to the lapsed who possess martyr's certificates without waiting for the decision of the bishop. That is, at the daily offering (what we call the Lord's Supper) they receive their gifts, present their offerings for them, and let them take part in their whole celebration and in the Eucharistic meal.[8]

The situation becomes clearer when we look at Alexandria. There the martyrs gave prayer and table communion to the penitent lapsed, and Bishop Dionysius asks his Antioch colleague whether he will indorse this.[9] There (in Alexandria) the bishop had no right to decide the case himself. The martyr-libellus was sufficient. The bishop followed as a matter of course. This gives us a clear view of the old Church practice. There was no formal solemn declaration of the martyrs and of other pneumatics; they simply get the conviction that

---

[7] Ep. 14 (5), 4. Müller, p. 85, note 2.
[8] 15 (10), 1; 16 (9), 2; and other passages. See
[9] Eusebius vi, 42.

God has forgiven the penitent sinners, and so communion was naturally opened to them.[10]

Compare now the behavior of the Carthaginian presbyters. They disown the right of the bishop to decide, and took it upon themselves. Their behavior is therefore a dishonor to the episcopate, and a despisal of his priesthood and of his chair.[11] That is, they act as was customary at Alexandria at that time. But their behavior appears in a different light to Cyprian, because the right of the bishop had developed otherwise in Carthage than it had in Alexandria. Callistus's exaltation of the bishop had struck home more deeply in Carthage. But the presbyters at length come around. They break off communion with the lapsed.[12] They confess that their decision is only for the time being, and that in any case the bishop had to decide. The opposition therefore could not have been as heavy as it has been represented. At the bottom they did not oppose Cyprian's episcopal rights as he conceived them. They only waived them at the start If they belonged to an older generation who had known other ways in the persecution of Septimius Severus (reigned 193-211), their conduct is quite natural.

---

[10] Sohm agrees with this. [11] Ep. 17 (11). [12] Ep. 20 (14), 2.

Still there were presbyters whose opposition went deeper—especially Fortunatus and Novatus. For the latter, who was on the lax side at Carthage and the strict side in Rome, it was probably opposition to Cyprian himself.[13] They even wrote to Rome to urge denial of all communion to Cyprian.[14] Cyprian defends himself to the satisfaction, it seems to me, of all impartial students.[15]

Probably Novatus was the leading spirit in this irreconcilable opposition, who worked on the sympathies of his colleagues for former customs,—those "good old times," perhaps, when the bishops did not loom so high.

We come now to the lapsed. They stormed the confessors and martyrs, as we have seen, and received libelli by the thousand. But their hopes were all dashed to the ground when the presbyters withdrew the communion they had first granted. This created a critical situation. All the lapsed without exception had received letters of peace from the confessors,—a gross abuse of privilege. The lapsed cried aloud for the communion promised. In the provinces the pressure was so great that the bishops gave in, at least in part. In Carthage the clergy

---

[13] See Cyprian's portrayal of this old hate in Epistle 43 (39), 1.
[14] If we may so interpret what is back of Epistle 20 (14).
[15] Ep. 20 (14).

wavered. Cyprian must meet them half way. Informed of the difficult position of the clergy, Cyprian concluded to concede something. On his own initiative he wrote saying that in the prospect of death peace could be granted to those who could show martyr's certificates, that is, they would be received into full communion with the Church.[16] That was the standpoint that the Roman society had taken at the beginning of the persecution, only without having regard to martyr's certificates. In fact, in Rome the martyrs and confessors would have nothing to do with the lapsed.

Cyprian made no further concessions, the African bishops assented to his principles, Rome came out in the same way, and most of the lapsed quieted themselves.[17] A part, however, remained defiant. The martyr Paul had given them peace; they had it therefore already in heaven; let the Church give it also, to which they already belonged in a true sense.[18] It will be seen from this that if the dissatisfied lapsed attach themselves to the dissatisfied presbyters, we have the materials for a new Church in Carthage.

And so we come to the so-called schism of Felicissimus,—a dark corner in Church history, though

---

[16] Ep. 18 (1a).　　[17] 32 (31), 2.　　[18] 33 (26); 35 (28); and 36 (29), 1.

Karl Müller has thrown welcome light into it. About March, 251, the persecution over, Cyprian prepared to go back to Carthage. The confessors had not yet dared to assemble in full public meeting. Only three presbyters are faithful from Cyprian's point of view; the others are either scattered or as untrustworthy as a part of the society. Some of the lapsed are still in revolt. Cyprian sends therefore a commission of two bishops and one or two Carthaginian presbyters to attend to some things before he ventures himself. They are to distribute financial help from the Church treasury to the needy, particularly to those who need help in business, making careful inquiry as to conditions, worthiness, etc. They are also to note the able and faithful in the Church, and those who are eligible to Church office. No sooner is the commission at work than Felicissimus steps out against them and threatens the brethren who applied for aid, that, if they take the money and obey the bishops, he would not permit them to communicate even on deathbed. A part then fell back, but the majority took the money.

Why this passionate interference of Felicissimus? And why did a part of the society hold with him?

With the expected return of the bishop it was

a fitting time for the opposition to come to a head. Otherwise the investigations of the commission might overawe and their subventions win. Besides, as soon as Cyprian returns, he will begin a careful inquiry into each case of the lapsed. Will this investigation be favorable? Will those who rushed to the tribunals to deny Christ shine well beside those who were overcome by torture? But both classes had already received letters of peace from the martyrs or in their name. Look at the hardness of the bishop in going behind the letters to weigh each case! This is the moment, therefore, to assert their rights, and standing on the prerogative of the martyrs, claim their place in the Church.

It is probable that Felicissimus was only a spokesman for the five presbyters who are always seen at his side. And as a prominent layman—there is no evidence for the common idea that he was a deacon at this time—it may have been supposed that he would influence the lay members to revolt. Cyprian acted with promptness. He sent word to the commission to exclude Felicissimus, another layman, Augendus, and any others who held with them, from the Church. This they did. Therefore the schism.

Hitherto it had been largely a layman's movement. Now the five presbyters came out boldly on the side of Felicissimus, some of whom had communicated with the lapsed. They now open the doors of communion to this class. They lead the lapsed to destruction, says Cyprian.[19] They slight the decree of Cyprian and of the Roman clergy and confessors, as well as all the bishops of this and of the other side of the sea. They create a new sacrilegious tradition. They erect another altar, a new priesthood. So they separate themselves from the Church, for in it is only one altar, that of the bishop. The latter need not exclude them: they have excluded themselves before all the world.

Did the presbyters and Felicissimus so think? Evidently not. After the martyrs have granted forgiveness to the penitent lapsed, they really have peace in heaven, and no bishop is justified in forbidding another to hold communion with them. That is, the presbyters really place themselves upon the old standpoint of the precatholic time when the charismatic ministry, the prophets and apostles, who spoke in the Holy Ghost, were still living forces in the world. Their voice was now heard, so to speak, in the martyrs, who had shown by their heroic testimony that they had succeeded to the spiritual

---

[19] Ep. 43 (39).

power of apostles. Whatsoever they bind or loose on earth is bound or loosed in heaven. Cyprian's attempt to tie this prerogative to an official class, the bishops, evidently made no impression on some of the older generation in Carthage. It is the old story of the prophet against the priest. But one part was struggling against, the other for, the current of the age, and that makes all the difference in the world as to success or failure, though not as to right or wrong.

But the new Church continued. Felicissimus was ordained deacon. Cyprian returned on or after Easter, 251, and therewith ceases his correspondence with the society. A great synod was held in Carthage in 251 to deliberate on the question. It excommunicated Felicissimus and the five presbyters, and as to the lapsed decided (1) that there should be a careful examination of each case; (2) that the lapsed who had not sacrificed, such, for instance, as the *thurificati* or those who only burned or threw incense to the emperor's image or at the altars of the gods, and such as had bought certificates from the officers,—that these could be restored to full membership after penance and public application to the bishop; (3) that the *sacrificati* should be restored at the hour of death, if they continued penitent; (4)

but that those who showed penitence only in sickness or at approaching death should be refused.[20] This was certainly a sensible middle way,—keeping something of the former strictness, and yet conceding a good deal to the actual facts and to the necessities of souls. It will be noticed that the bishop's prerogative is fully secured, and that the martyr's libelli are left out in the cold. The day of the bishop had fully come.

Why this strictness to those who sacrificed, however, and tenderness to the rest of the lapsed? Were they sinners above all others? It was impossible that a compromise like that, however well meaning and on the whole just, should stand, especially in a time when a fresh persecution might at any moment bring penitent lapsed to the jaws of death. The Church must either go back to the second century conception of remissible and irremissible sins, or go back farther to the apostolic conception of the pardonableness of all sins, except such as from their nature reveal a heart deliberately and irrecoverably given to evil.[21] But the Church does not know the heart, and all she can act on is the presumption of the genuineness of the penitence. The main question with the Christian is not, Has he sinned? The

---
[20] Ep. 54 (50), and especially 55 (51).
[21] See Matt. xii, 31-2; Heb. x, 26-31; 1 John v, 16-7.

affirmative may be assumed, at least for sins of thought, neglect, inadvertence. The real question is, Is he truly penitent? The Church can not go back of that record, even if she has to follow her Master in His staggering severities.[22] We need not be surprised, therefore, if a year or two later a second synod, in view of a threatening persecution, gave peace to *all* the lapsed, who had kept themselves to the Church and had faithfully done penance. This was coming round to the position of the presbyters and Felicissimus, though for another reason and by another road. But these continued their independent action, had Fortunatus consecrated bishop of Carthage, sent an embassy to Rome to win recognition there, and kept up their Church for some time. How long we do not know. The movement had no reason for existence after the action of the second Cyprianic council, and apparently died a natural death soon after that. With such a bishop as Cyprian to pass on questions of the lapsed, it was just as well that it died.

Now as to the results. We see how Cyprian changed. First, he was disinclined to grant peace to the lapsed. Then he was willing to grant it to the dying who had martyr's letters. After that

---

[22] Matt. xviii, 22.

when his first council left martyrs and confessors entirely out of the account, and decided that whole classes of lapsed should have peace during life, Cyprian agreed, as he did finally when the second council decided that all could have peace. Why was this? Evidently it was because each advance left the bishop more and more in possession of the field.

Notice the development of the Church generally. Formerly the martyrs had the right to give communion to those whose sins they forgave, or of whom they said, in virtue of their possession of the Spirit, that God had forgiven. But that did not compel the society to take in the offender, it only enabled it to do so. Where the bishop had to decide as to the participation in the Eucharistic sacrifice, no sinner could come to that offering without his consent. (Customs may have varied more or less in different cities.) But that did not mean that the bishop had the initiative alone, and that the judgment of a martyr might remain in suspense. The society itself or a part of it could grant communion to a fallen brother on a martyr's claim, and with their weight press the bishop to a favorable action. Only the last decision remained with the bishop, because he presided at the offering.

In all this Callistus, as far as we know, was the first to make a change. He left the martyrs out, and shoved in between them and the society the decision of the bishop. Their claim has no power till the bishop indorses it. This principle was adopted at once in the West, at least in Carthage. Still some sections in the Church held to the old practice, as the presbyters in Carthage, and the lapsed grasped so eagerly at it that they expected the bishop and the society without more ado to govern themselves according to the letters of the martyrs. But their fate was sealed, because the latter never once put in an absolute claim of deciding their admission. That they left to the bishops and congregation.

Cyprian was victor. He advances, martyrs disappear, the bishop alone is left. Finally, the bishop can go his own way, if necessary, even in spite of the will of the congregation. With that is reached the first step that can be called Catholic in the full sense. History is being made with a vengeance. No mortal sin excludes: adultery, murder, apostasy—all can be fixed up in the regular penitential institution of the Church.

In the East, however, the old conditions remained for some time. In Alexandria, about 250, the bishop had no clearly defined right to visé the decision or pardon of a martyr, nor was it customary. As late as the Diocletian persecution (303 ff) the martyrs played a similar rôle in that city, as they did in Carthage in 250. But these are only unessential fragments of a time forever flown.[23]

---

[23] Prof. Karl Müller, whom I have followed in this exposition. See note, p. 84.

CHAPTER IX.

THE NOVATIAN CHURCH.

If the Felicissimus movement in Carthage, growing out of the disciplinary and penitential controversy in which Cyprian had such a large share, came to nothing, so far as a separate Church was concerned, that can not be said of a movement that sprang from the same cause in Rome, of which the letters of Cyprian are our chief contemporary information. That spread from Rome west to Spain and east to Syria, and continued a separate and distinct Church life Catholic in essentials and orthodox for five centuries. This had so close a relation to movements in which Cyprian was a chief actor that a brief statement concerning it is in place. It is one of the most significant outgrowths of the Cyprianic age.

We have already seen that in the second and early part of the third century it was customary to exclude definitely and finally from the Church those guilty of idolatry, adultery, and related sins, and murder, reserving for the penitents of this class the

THE NOVATIAN CHURCH. 103

mercy of God in the next world. This shows clearly that at that time the Church was not thought of as coextensive with salvation; that is, one might be saved and yet not be a member of the Church. This strict exclusion was broken up by the Roman bishop, Callistus (218-23), who made an exception of sins of impurity, though alleviations were permitted by the custom of honoring martyrs' intercessions and forgiveness. It is evident that in Cyprian's time absolution for gross sins of the flesh was not uncommon.[1] One of the consequences of Callistus's looseness was the separate Church of Hippolytus in Rome. But as the Hippolytan Church had already amalgamated with the general Church before 250, there had probably been a sharpening of discipline by Callistus's successors. This does not mean that fleshly sinners were finally excluded in Rome, for absolution for such sins was no longer a matter of controversy there. As to idolatry—that was another matter.

The Decian persecution changed the whole situation. The number of the lapsed was so great that to keep up the old rule imperiled the existence of congregations. Even Tertullian seemed to feel that overstrictness in some cases here might be unjust,

---
[1] Ep. 4 (61); 55 (51), 20.

for in torture one might deny the faith as it were involuntarily, while keeping it unspotted in his heart.[2] Besides, the doctrine of the Church demanded a change. If the Church is the hierarchy, "outside of which there is no salvation," then the old belief is deceptive that God could receive the penitent sinner to grace to whom the Church had denied absolution. There is no doubt that the Decian persecution greatly helped this theory. Would it be merciful to relegate vast masses of penitents to the uncovenanted mercies of God, when their reception again into the Church might make their salvation certain? Besides, it was the custom almost universal in 250 to give remission just before death. Why not make assurance doubly sure? Who knows when death may come? Why keep the penitent in this miserable uncertainty? If the Church forgives, they are forgiven. "The longing of the lapsed after reconciliation, the insecurity as to salvation where Churchly absolution failed, even with earnest penitence,[3] shows most distinctly that the Church was forced by her laity to hold herself as the indispensable condition of salvation."[4] It

---

[2] De Pud. 22.   [3] Eus. 6, 44.

[4] Harnack, art. on Novatianism in the Hauck-Herzog, 3. Aufl. XIV, 223-42 (1904). Harnack has gone into this matter with characteristic German thoroughness, but with his own lucidity, and I follow his conclusions in this chapter.

was carrying this theory out to its logical result, the theory that the Church, through her officers, has the power of the keys, that she opens or shuts the kingdom of heaven, and that only those to whom she opens go in,—it was this thoroughly Cyprianic theory which at the bottom caused by way of protest the great Novatian Church.

Novatian was a presbyter of the Roman Church, one of the holiest and ablest of her clergy. He was the only theologian of the Roman Church for three centuries. He was learned, eloquent, and a thinker, and it has been left to recent research to restore to his name some books which Catholic copyists later either could not or would not assign to their real author—him whom they looked upon as a schismatic—but knew it was perfectly safe to father upon Cyprian. Could an arch-schismatic write such books as those on the "Spectacles," on "Modesty," on the "Praise of Martyrdom," on the "Jews?" Horrors! Never! Put them down to Cyprian! The poverty of the Roman Church in learning and theological power is a striking fact in the history of the early Church. Her uninstructed presbyters when they write letters to Carthage, printed in Cyprian, can not command decent Latin. Therefore during the fifteen months' vacancy in the chair after the martyrdom of Fabian (January 20, 250), when the government of the Church reverted according to the primitive custom to the presbyters with the laity, their literary spokesman was Novatian. He conducted the correspondence of the society. "A maintainer of the Gospel and of Christ," Cyprian scornfully calls him—Cyprian was a dealer in sarcasm—after he became the leader of an independent Church.[5] His conduct was blameless, and even his enemies can charge nothing against him. The presbyter college in Rome, when not decimated by persecution, consisted of fifty-three persons,[6] and at their head in moral weight after the death of Fabian stood Novatian, while of their next bishop, Cornelius, we hear nothing.

We have three letters of the Roman presbyters in Cyprian (other letters are lost), of which two are by Novatian.[7] In the first it is said that it is the custom to give absolution to the sick penitent lapsed, a custom which Cyprian now follows implicitly,[8] though at first he was stricter. In Epistle 30, written by Novatian, the practice followed by Cyprian is praised, and, with all strictness against the libellatici, the possibility of a reception again

---

[5] Ep. 44 (40), 3.   [6] Eus. 6: 43, 11.   [7] Eps. 8 (2) in uncouth **Latin**, and 30 and 36 (29) by Novatian.   [8] See Eps. 18 (12); 19 (13); 20 (14), 3.

THE NOVATIAN CHURCH.

into the Church is not cut off. When peace is restored, the matter of the lapsed shall be treated in a great council. Until that time let them show a proper penitence. "We will pray that upon the penitence of the lapsed the effect of the pardon shall follow, and that they in knowledge of their transgression shall prove their patience in the meantime."[9] This middle path, he says, we have followed in common with some neighboring bishops and those present in Rome. No new practice shall be introduced, not at least till a bishop is elected. In the other epistle, Novatian shows perfect agreement with Cyprian, and strongly supports him in his conflict with lax confessors and their letters of peace. So the letters which Cyprian sends to Roman confessors show harmony both in Rome itself and between Cyprian and Rome.[10] Up to the beginning of spring, 251, therefore, there was no sign of an independent Church in Rome. While Novatian was characterized by the moral earnestness and decision with which he asserted evangelical vigor and a robust faith, he did not differ materially from Cyprian and the Church of his time as to dealing with the lapsed.

Like a thunderbolt out of a clear sky all this is

---

[9] Ep. 30, 6.   [10] Eps. 28 (24); 31 (25); 37 (15).

changed. In March, 251, after the Decian persecution stopped, Cornelius, a novice who had been clothed with all the clerical offices one after the other, was elected bishop of Rome by the majority. But the minority, consisting among others of at least five presbyters and the most honored confessors, immediately elected Novatian bishop, and had him ordained according to the ordinary custom by three bishops. There we have the start of the second independent Catholic Church in Rome.[11] Why was this?

It has been shown by Harnack that formally and on the surface the difference that caused the movement was a purely personal one. The presbyters and confessors simply did not like Cornelius; they distrusted him; they had no respect for him. But they had perfect confidence in Novatian and respected him profoundly. It has been one of the frequent mistakes revealed by Church history,—the election of men to high office who do not command the entire respect of all whose duty calls them to judge.

---

[11] The view of some old Protestant writers and some modern Baptists that the Novatian Church was a reaction in favor of primitive Christianity is not well founded. As to moral discipline, it was stricter than the general Church, and its idea as to the power of the keys more spiritual; but in nearly all its customs and doctrines it did not differ one iota from the main Church. This is admitted by the eminent Baptist scholar, Prof. Albert Henry Newman, in his Church History, I, 207 (1900).

THE NOVATIAN CHURCH.

But the personal objection was unconsciously mixed up with another partly personal, partly theoretical. During the persecution and after, Cornelius's behavior was not entirely above suspicion. Even if the accusation that he was a libellaticus was unfounded, he had been in communion with bishops who had offered to idols, especially with Trophimus, who had given up strict discipline.[12] Cornelius, therefore, notoriously represented a lax discipline, and he was therefore unacceptable to the stricter members of the society. The majority elected him (as Harnack well says) in the interest of self-preservation, believing that he would govern mildly. It is evident also that Novatian was not himself the inciter to the second Church,—but was pressed into it. "If thou against thy will," says Dionysius of Alexandria in his letter to him, "as thou sayest, have been carried along, then prove it by coming freely back again."[13] More easily said than done. The matter went deeper than Dionysius thought. Over against the threatening loose rule under the slippery Cornelius, Novatian decided to emphasize again the old penitential discipline, and to admit exceptions no more. Starting with personal dislike, the thing went forward to material

---

[12] Ep. 55 (51), 10.   [13] Eus. 6, 45.

differences. It was an eternal lesson to the Church to elect men as pastors and bishops upon whom all can unite in respect and love. "If one considers," says Harnack, "how for a long time in the East and West the lax and strict practice existed peacefully together (even after the Novatian Church) without any schism until far on into the fourth century and even longer, if we remember that at the beginning Cyprian always blames the *fact* of the schism not the *theory* of the schismatics, one can not doubt that the differences would have been borne with farther by both sides if they had not been poisoned in one and the same congregation by irreconcilable opposition between personalities."[14] On the other hand, as Harnack admits, the range which the Novatian movement took and its long duration show that the fundamental differences in principle were after all the chief ones.

Now what attitude did Cyprian take to this movement? If it is evident that the lofty character and theological attainments of Novatian and the naturally rather strict views of the Carthaginian would have won him completely to Novatian's side if it had not been for two things. The first was the situation in Carthage itself. On account of the

---

[14] In Hauck-Herzog, 3. Aufl. XIV, 233.

THE NOVATIAN CHURCH. 111

open schism of Felicissimus, Cyprian had been compelled to yield so far as to grant the taking in again of the lapsed.[15] He was veering more and more to moderate views on this. Second, his Church views made recognition of Novatian impossible. The Church is clergy and laity gathered around one lawfully elected bishop. There could be no more two bishops in one city, in one local Church, than there could be two heads on one man. To hold to one bishop is the essence of Christianity. Since Cornelius was lawfully elected, he is the God-appointed head of the Roman Church, and not to gather with him is to gather with the adversary, Satan. That there could be two independent Churches in Rome, one in love and loyalty to Christ, one in faith, hope, and charity, but with different discipline, different government, different heads independent of each other but not independent of the Church and of Christ,—that is a thought that never entered Cyprian's head, or, if it did, to be repudiated instantly. He was too much a child of the third century for that. But it is evident that the strictly Catholic evolution had not gone so far that it had carried every one to his position. If it had, the greatest spirit in the Roman Church in the third

---
[15] Ep. 43 (39), esp. §§ 2, 6.

century would not have allowed himself to be elected as a bishop of the Roman Church, nor would presbyters, confessors, and laymen have united in electing him. For the previous legal election of Cornelius was incontestable.

But the majority were with him who had the seat. At a great Roman synod where there were sixty bishops and many presbyters and deacons,[16] Novatian was excommunicated, and penance only (not lifelong exclusion) proclaimed for *all* the fallen. Novatian tried by letters and embassies to win recognition from brother bishops. Nor was he altogether unsuccessful. Fabius of Antioch favored him, and numerous synods at least did not disown him. Not so Cyprian. He wrote to the Roman confessors trying to call them off from the schism, so called, which as usual he covered with opprobrious epithets.[17] I might have added to the two reasons which led Cyprian to oppose Novatian a third, viz., that his enemy in Carthage, the presbyter Novatus, who had been one of the chief supporters of Felicissimus, went to Rome and instead of favoring the lax side of Cornelius, as he naturally would if his principle had not been, Anything to beat Cyprian, he went over to the camp of Novatian, and did what

[16] Eus., 6, 43. [17] Ep. 46 (43).

The Novatian Church.

he could to help him and hurt Cornelius and Cyprian. Is it any wonder that Cyprian stood by Cornelius?

Novatus makes the Carthaginian furious. He attacks him with all his accustomed venom, perhaps more. Novatus is "always greedy of novelty, raging with insatiable avarice, inflated with arrogance and stupidity of swelling pride; always known with bad repute to the bishops; always condemned by the voice of all the priests as a heretic and perfidious; always inquisitive that he may betray; flatters that he may deceive; never faithful that he may love; a torch and a fire to blow up the flames of sedition, a whirlwind and tempest to make shipwrecks of the faith; the foe of quiet," etc. "Orphans despoiled by him, widows defrauded, moneys of the Church withheld; his father died of hunger in the street, and left unburied. The womb of his wife was smitten by a blow of his heel, and in the miscarriage that followed the offspring was brought forth, the fruit of the father's murder."[18] That's Cyprian. I wonder how much of this was personal hatred of an opponent, the exaggerated rhetoric of the advocate, and how much the actual description of a scoundrel priest. In the first case it is a bad

---

[18] Ep. 52 (48), 2.

reflection on Cyprian; in the second, it is a worse reflection on the Church. But it is inconceivable how a man of Novatus's reputation, as Cyprian described it, could exert the influence he did in Rome, according to Cyprian's account, who makes him the chief cause of the Novatian movement.[19] Anyhow, as Harnack says, the solidarity between Cornelius and Cyprian received its strongest seal in the common opposition against Novatus.

Cyprian now tried to win the Roman confessors from the side of Novatian. He succeeded. Cornelius wrote to him that the glorious confessors, Maximus and his companions, had forsaken Novatian and returned to the Church, and that they had said that they had been deceived by the malice, cunning, lies, perjury, and wolflike friendship of the deceiving and crafty beast, the schismatic and heretical Novatian.[20] But when the confessors themselves came to tell to Cyprian the story of their leaving Novatian they practically make Cornelius a liar, as they allege no faults in Novatian, but simply their concern for the welfare of the Church. They say: "We are certain, dearest brother, that you also rejoice together with us with equal ear-

---

[19] The Liberian Catalogue does the same. It says: "At that time Novatus came over from Africa, and separated Novatian and certain persons from the Church." [20] Ep. 49 (45).

nestness that we having taken advice, and especially considering the interests of peace of the Church, having passed by all other matters, and reserved them to God's judgment, have made peace with Cornelius, our brother, as well as with the whole clergy."[21] Here they hinted at heavy objections to Cornelius, but they have been persuaded for the sake of unity to waive them, leave them to a Higher Judgment. In order to confirm them, Cyprian writes and sends them a copy of his great book on the "Unity of the Church," on which a word later.

Novatian did not give up his cause, but sought all the more to push on the institution of new bishops.[22] A second embassy of Novatian agitators went to Carthage, among them Novatus himself, while Cornelius immediately sent his own people for counter effect, and characterized the others as transgressors and knaves. The Novatian embassy succeeded in gathering a society in Carthage, over which Maximus (not to be confounded with the confessor) was made bishop. There were now three independent Churches and bishops in Carthage—Cyprian, Fortunatus (Felicissimus), and Maximus, representing the moderate, the lax, and

---

[21] Ep. 53 (49). [22] 55 (51), 24.

the strict theories of discipline, but all being alike Catholic in doctrine and polity. But Cyprian, in spite of all his passionateness against the "lax,"[23] had to make more concessions, which, of course, sharpened the opposition of the Novatian Church. These concessions were the forebodings of the action of the Carthaginian council of May, 253, when under the threatening clouds of the new persecution, that of Gallus, it was decided that all the penitent lapsed should be immediately received.[24] A sensible decision, say we of to-day, but what a fall from the olden times. One of the reasons for this decision was alleged to be visions and revelations,[25] to which Cyprian, no doubt with absolute honesty and perhaps truth, laid claim, and which reminds me of the "private wire" of my late lamented colleague, Professor Samuel F. Upham, who used to say in his inimitably droll way, "Brethren, beware of the man who has a private wire to heaven." The council, however, did not renounce the communion with bishops who still kept up the old practice, only threatening them with the judgment of God for their strictness. They evidently did not want to make it necessary (says Harnack) for any one to go over to the Novatian camp.

---

[23] Ep. 59 (54), 12.   [24] 57 (53).   [25] Ibid. §§ 2, 5.

THE NOVATIAN CHURCH. 117

The persecution of Gallus was not really as severe as was feared. Nevertheless it gave opportunity for many of the lapsed in the Decian to witness a courageous confession, and thus show the genuineness of their penitence and standing as Christians. By the banishment of Cornelius it enabled his friends to celebrate him as a confessor, and they now said that God himself had legitimated him over against Novatian. The latter henceforth drops out of the Cyprianic letters. Many bishops kept up the strict practice without joining Novatian. At the great council of Antioch, though Novatian was acknowledged as bishop, the loose practice won the day. While some Churches came back to the so-called Catholic Church, the Novatian movement spread over Egypt, Asia Minor, Syria, Arabia, even as far as Mesopotamia, and at the beginning had great success.[26]

At the bottom what was the difference between the parties? What did the Novatian Church stand for? While at the start Novatian did not differ materially from Cyprian, he came back under the stress of the lax drift and from aversion to the person and views of Cornelius to the older view which limited the power of the keys to remissible sins. He

---

[26] Eus. 7, 5; Ep. 55 (51), 24.

went on to explain Matt. x, 32-33 as the kernel of the Gospel, therefore to deny absolution in any case to one who had lapsed into heathenism; while the most conservative of the other party allowed absolution to the penitent in view of death, to be followed soon by a much more general application of the mercy of the Church. Understand that Novatian did not deny eternal salvation to the lapsed on the strength of Matt. x, 33, nor deny the efficacy of penitence, but said only that the Scriptures left the decision to God, and the Church had no right to anticipate this judgment and grant absolution in cases reserved to Himself. Harnack makes the whole question come to this: What is the Church and what are her powers? If she is the indispensable institute of salvation to the extent that out of her no one can be saved (Cyprian), then it is fearful cruelty to deny to any penitent admission some time before death. Cyprian's doctrine of the Church must inevitably lead to generous dealings with all sinners, and we see in the so-called Catholic Churches to-day (Roman, Anglican, Greek, Russian, Armenian, etc.). Cyprian did not say, of course, that all in the Church would be saved, only that none outside of her would be. On the other hand, if the Church is the institute of salvation in the sense that she has the Gospel, the means of grace, etc., but that salvation is not absolutely bound up with her, that God still works outside of her, then leaving apostates outside, while giving them prayers, sympathy, exhortation, etc., is not cruelty, because they can still be saved. And the Church will not for these sinners go beyond the Word.

Besides, the Cyprianic and soon the general Church theory means, as I have just hinted, a liberal interpretation of the parable of the wheat and the tares. The Church is not the society of the saints, of the elect, but she is the ground on which they grow. Her religious character is represented, not by the character of her members, but by her possession of the keys, of sacramental absolution, of ordination, of exclusive grace. These are indispensable to salvation, but they do not guarantee salvation. But she instructs for salvation, and stimulates to virtue, and only in her has virtue any worth from God.[27] All this meant further externalizing, for we have to tell the inquirer where the Church is. This led to the priesthood, especially to the episcopate, which in its unity guarantees the legitimacy of the Church. So every schism becomes in effect a heresy,—an advance beyond Irenæus and

---

[27] Ep. 54 (50); 57 (53), 4.

Tertullian. On the other hand, Novatian said, the Church must exclude great sinners; she can not absolve idolators, but must refer their case to God, who alone has the power to forgive such sins.[28] "It is not necessary," he said, "to have peace from the bishops in order to share in the glory of the martyrs, —greater peace is to be received through the authority of the Lord."[29] He believed also that mortal sin in any member of the society stains in a sense the whole Church.[30] The Church's formal forgiveness is not necessary to salvation; God reserves some authority to Himself. The chief matter is union with Christ. The Church must be really what she is ostensibly,—a Church of saints.

To an evangelical Christian the Novatian movement must look as a well-meant but belated and vain effort to "save the face" of primitive Christianity in an ill-timed emphasis on second-century features of pentitential discipline by those who knew apostolic Christianity almost as little as their opponents. Both were Catholic, not evangelical. If the Church must be Catholic, perhaps the bishops were as wise as Novatian. The greatest transformation Christianity ever underwent—that from the Gospel of faith and love of the first century to the hierarchical

---

[28] Soc. 4, 28.   [29] Ep. 57 (53), 4.   [30] 55 (51), 27.

and sacramental Catholicism of the second and third—that transformation the bishops carried through, Harnack thinks, with moderation and discretion. And if that transformation was an historical necessity, back current eddies like Novatian's, the Donatist, etc., were as futile as they were illogical. Still they are interesting as reminders of another and truer age.

CHAPTER X.

MERCY AND HELP.

The glory of ancient Christianity was as much its love as its faith. The love was the fruit of the faith and showed its genuineness and its power. This was the talisman which opened the hearts of many pagans: Behold how these Christians love one another. An instance or two of this in Cyprian's life shows that great bishop and Christian in his most attractive light.

The barbaric tribes who were driven back from the fertile coast line of Africa by the Romans were never entirely subdued, but ever and anon made raids on the peaceful settlements,—prophecy of the coming time when Vandal and Saracen would sweep away African Christianity and the civilization which went with it. "In the year 252 there was a concentrated general advance. Mauretania felt them. They broke out of Aures through the grand chain of fortress settlements, harassing the domains of the strongest towns, Thubunæ in the salt marsh, and

Mercy and Help. 123

the vast soldier colony of Lambæsis. From the Sahara they came right through the province itself into the terebinth woods of Tucca and to the great center of traffic, Assuras, little more than a hundred miles from Carthage. The Christian population of at least eight sees was thus lacerated."[1] It was principally the women and children whom the Berbers thus kidnaped.

These Berber raids seem in real cruelty to have been child's play beside the Turkish massacres of Bulgarians in 1876 and of Armenians in 1895, but they were sufficiently devastating. As to kidnaping, that is an old practice which seems indigenous to those Eastern lands, of which our own generation has had reminders in the cases of the accomplished and devoted Miss Stone, kidnaped by revolutionists restive under Turkish misrule in 1901, and the American Perdicaris, kidnaped by a Mohammedan insurrectionary chief in this same Mauretania in 1904, when we had Roosevelt's famous message, "Perdicaris alive or Raisuli dead!"

The redeeming of captives was not specifically a Christian virtue. Cicero praises it as especially becoming senators: "That benignity is useful to

---

[1] Benson, 236-7. Benson is wonderfully careful and accurate in all geographical, antiquarian, and legal information.

the State by which captives are redeemed from slavery, and the poor are enriched. That it was the common custom with our order we see copiously described in the speech of Crassus. This kind of bounty I prefer far before the munificent exhibition of shows. That is the part of grave men and of great, this of flatterers of the populace."[2] But it is doubtful how much pure benevolence in the Christian sense there was in this, or whether it was not something like the modern practice of exchanging prisoners of war. At any rate in rescuing the Berber captives everybody contributed, rich and poor—the spontaneous pouring out of affection for those in distress. In the Church of Carthage about one hundred thousand sesterces (about $4,000) were contributed,—an enormous sum for a Church just decimated by persecution, which always meant confiscation of property, as well as the imprisonment, banishment, or death of bread-winners. It shows, however, the tremendous hold Christianity had gotten on all classes of society—not less among the rich—in the third century.

An interesting letter is that which Cyprian sends with the contribution.[3] The cold lawyer of heathen-

---

[2] De Officiis, 2, 18. The liberal "redeem those captured by robbers," etc. (2, 16).   [3] Ep. 62 (59).

ism, whose old sternness had not left him, however, in dealing with men of his own faith who had left his kind of unity, has been transformed by the beautiful spirit of Christian piety. "With excessive grief and with tears, dearest brethren, I have read your letter, which, from the solicitude of your love, you wrote to me concerning the captivity of your brethren and sisters." He then quotes the fine passages of Paul, 1 Cor. xii, 26, 2 Cor. xi, 29, and says: "The captivity of our brethren must be reckoned our captivity, and the grief of those in danger our grief, since indeed there is one body of our union; and not love only, but religion ought to instigate and strengthen us to redeem the members of the brethren." He then refers to the possible fate of women and girls, and adds: "Our brotherhood considering all these things according to your letter, and sorrowfully examining, have all promptly and willingly and liberally gathered together supplies of money for the brethren, being indeed always according to the strength of their faith prone to the work of God, but now once more stimulated to salutary works by consideration of so great a suffering, we have then sent you a sum of one hundred thousand sesterces, which have been collected here in the Church over which, by the Lord's mercy, we preside, by the contributions of the clergy and people established with us, which you will there dispense with what diligence you may." He deprecates the coming of such a calamity again, but says that if it should come the Church in Carthage "will willingly and liberally render help." He encloses separately the names of contributors, especially "of my colleagues and fellow-priests," and asks the Numidian Church to remember them in prayer.

Perhaps a severer test was the terrible plague which visited Africa in 252. It was a kind of malignant typhoid fever, complicated with other horrible symptoms or diseases. Nothing tests fidelity to altruistic ideals better than a fearful visitation like this. Modern Christendom hardly knows what this means, though India and Ireland have known famine; and occasionally tropical diseases, the offspring of insanitary living and effluvia of the accumulated filth of ages, have struck civilized lands, (*e. g.*, yellow fever, New Orleans, 1878, 1905.) The last time a great plague spread from the east and south as far north as England was in 1663-5, though portions of Europe were devastated more than once in the eighteenth century, and parts of the East frequently in the nineteenth. The fatality of these epidemics is something awful, the Black

Death of 1348-50 carrying away, it is said, a quarter of the population of Europe. We need not be surprised, then, at the agony and mortal terror of pagan populations when such a specter stepped into their midst. Those that could fled to uninfected places or anywhere to escape the dread disease. They left their sick behind, or thrust them out of their houses to die in the streets, and left their dead bodies unburied.

> "Before mine eyes in opposition sits
> Grim death, my son and foe."

What a commentary on that generous and beautiful paganism some of our moderns praise!

For twenty years this plague went to and fro through Mediterranean lands. It came back to Alexandria in 261 and in four years it had reduced the population one-half. It was the ally of the Persian in his war with the Roman Emperor Valerian, for it slew more Romans than his sword. In 262 five thousand died in Rome, and—if the historian Trebellius Pollio is considered correct—the same number in Achaia in a single day! Is it any wonder that to contemporaries it seemed the darkest misery that every visited mankind?

The heathen struck coins and raised altars to

"Healthful Apollo" (Apollo Salutaris). But their effective remedy has just been mentioned,—flights, desertions, barred gates, assassinations, drugged possets, seizures of fortunes of the sick and dying. Let the simple story of Cyprian's Deacon Pontius tell how both sides met the "hateful disease" which invaded every house in succession of the trembling populace, carrying off, day by day, with sudden attack, numberless people, every one from his own house. All were shuddering, fleeing, shunning the contagion, impiously exposing their own friends, as if with the shutting out of the person who was sure to die of the plague, one could shut out death itself. Meanwhile over the whole city there lay the carcasses of many, and by contemplation of a lot which in their turn would be theirs, demanded the pity of the passers-by for themselves. No one regarded anything but his cruel gains. No one trembled at the remembrance of a similar event. No one did to another what he wished for himself. In these circumstances it would be wrong to pass over what the pontiff of Christ (Cyprian) did, who excelled the pontiffs of the world in the love, as he did in the truth, of religion. As the people assembled together in one place he urged the benefits of mercy, teaching by example the same lessons how

Mercy and Help.

greatly the duties of benevolence avail to deserve well of God. Then he said that there was nothing wonderful in our cherishing our own people only with the needed attentions of love, but that he might become perfect who would do something more than the publicans and the heathen. He must overcome evil with good, practice a clemency like the divine clemency, love even his enemies, pray for his persecutors, as the Lord exhorts. God continually makes his sun to shine and sends showers upon aliens as well as His own. And if a man professes to be a son of God, why does he not imitate the example of his Father? It becomes us, he said, to answer to our birth (respondere natalibus), and it is not fitting that those who are evidently born of God should be degenerate, but rather that the propagation of a good Father should be proved in His offspring by the emulation of His goodness."[4]

The congregation responded nobly. They raised an abundant fund, formed a staff for nursing the sick, another for the burial of the dead, and covered the stricken city with a network of relief. What impression did this make upon the heathen? Apparently not very much. They were enraged because the Christians did not join in their offerings

---

[4] Vita Cyp. 9.

to Health, to Apollo, and to Cœlestis, Queen of Heaven (compare the offerings of Roman Catholics to Mary, Queen of Heaven, under similar and other circumstances). The populace clamored for the blood of the overseer, Cyprian, who was prompting the noblest relief for them. "To the lions," they called out in circus and amphitheater, and had him officially proscribed:[5] pagan to Cyprian, Jew to his Master after the raising of Lazarus.[6] Pontius speaks of his later banishment as a pagan recompense for benevolent civic activity, for his "withdrawing from living sight a horror like that of hell, for saving his country from becoming the empty shell of an exiled population."[7]

Cyprian's book, "Of Works and Alms," may be considered an echo of this great self-sacrifice of the Carthaginian Church. It is his philosophy of good deeds, his doctrine of merit. Is he here Catholic or Protestant? I think he does not belie his age nor himself. "God can be appeased by almsgiving alone."[8] "By works of righteousness God is satisfied, and with the deserts of mercy sins are cleansed."[9] He quotes the angel Raphael: "Prayer is good, and fasting, and alms; because alms also

---

[5] Ep. 54 (59), 6.   [6] John xi, 53.   [7] Vita Cyp. 11.
[8] De Opere et Eleemosynis, 4.   [9] Ibid. 5.

Mercy and Help. 131

doth deliver from death, and it purgeth away sins."[10] Prayer alone is of little avail unless it be made sufficient by good works. He takes Christ's words in Matt. xix, 21, as the law of the Gospel, and not simply the instruction which at that time the wise Teacher saw was best for the case before him. God "distributes to our merits and good works the promised rewards." "The Lord will never fail of giving a reward for our merits."[11]

On the other hand, the treatise "Of Works and Alms," is a noble plea for beneficence and good deeds. He strikes home upon those who by the "coveteousness of money do nothing for the fruit of their salvation," and he hopes that the "blush of dishonor and disgrace may strike upon their sordid consciences." He boldly represents Satan twitting Christ with the devotion of his (Satan's) followers, the rich gifts they give to Him, and the meanness of Christ's people. "Show, O Christ, such givers as these of Thine—those rich men, those men affluent with abounding wealth—whether in the Church wherein Thou presidest and beholdest they set forth a gift of that kind, having pledged or scattered their riches, yea having transferred them then by the change of their possessions for

---
[10] Tob. xii, 8, 9.   [11] De Op. et El. 26.

the better, into heavenly treasures! In those spectacles of mine, perishing and earthly as they are, no one is fed, no one is clothed, no one is sustained by the comfort of any meat or drink. All things between the madness of the exhibitor and the mistake of the spectator are perishing in a prodigal and foolish vanity of deceiving pleasures. There in thy poor thou art clothed and fed. Thou providest eternal life for those who labor for Thee, and scarcely are Thy people made equal to mine that perish, although they are honored by Thee with divine wages and heavenly rewards."[12] How beautiful his praise of charity: "An illustrious and divine thing is the saving labor of charity; a great comfort to believers, a wholesome guard of our security, a protection of hope, a safeguard of faith, a remedy for sin, a thing placed in the power of the doer, a thing both great and easy, a crown of peace without the risk of persecution; the true and greatest gift of God, needful for the weak, glorious for the strong, assisted by which the Christian accomplishes spiritual grace, deserves well of Christ the Judge, accounts God his debtor. For the palm of work of salvation let us gladly and readily strive, let us all in the struggle of righteousness run with God and Christ looking

---

[12] De Op. et El. 22.

Mercy and Help.

on. And let us who have already begun to be greater than this life and the world slacken our course by no desire of this life and of this world. If the day shall find us, whether it be the day of reward or of oppression, furnished, if swift, if running in this contest of charity, the Lord will never fail of giving a reward for our merits: in peace He will give to us who conquer a white crown for labor, in persecution a purple one for death."[13] We have here the words of a holy and devoted shepherd of souls, though of one steeped in Catholic ideas.

The sufferings which come to Christians and heathen brought up the two questions: (1) Why do calamities come to the world? and (2) Why do Christians suffer? It will be interesting to notice how these puzzling everlasting questions are answered by Cyprian.

In one of his most interesting books he takes up the first question. It seems that Demetrianus, proconsul of Africa, had charged upon the Christians that they were the cause of all the terrible plagues, etc., which were now falling upon the empire. This opinion of his lent zest to his persecuting measures. Cyprian meets it in this book "Ad Demetrianum" in two ways. First, he says that such things must be

---
[13] De Op. et El. 26.

expected in the old age of the world, when the forces of nature are drying up and all things hastening to a common ruin.[14] How foolish to impute to Christians what is due to nature. "No one should wonder that everything begins to fail in the world when the whole world itself is in process of failing, and in its end." Second, so far from calamities being punishments for Christians' impiety, they are direct punishments for heathen idolatry. All these natural evils—pestilence, disease, failure of crops, famine, etc.—are "in consequence of the sins which provoke them." They are all stripes of the Lord. The treatise is a terrific arraignment of the evils of the time, and a proof that Cyprian's hiding from persecution was not due to cowardice, for no coward could write in this strain. "You complain that the enemy rises up, as if, even though external arms and dangers from barbarians were repressed, the weapons of destructive assault, the calamities and wrongs of powerful citizens, would not be more ferocious and more harshly wielded within. You complain of barrenness and famine, as if drought made a greater famine than rapacity, as if the fierceness of want did not increase more terribly from grasping at the increase of the year's produce and

---

[14] This striking passage is inserted in the Hurst Ch. Hist. I, 198-9.

the accumulation of their price. You complain that the heaven is shut up from showers, although in the same way the barns are shut up on earth. You complain that now less is produced, as if what already had been produced is given to the indigent. You reproach plague and disease, while by plague itself or disease the crimes of individuals are either detected or increased, while mercy is not manifested to the weak, and avarice and rapine are waiting open-mouthed for the dead. The same men are timid in the duties of affection, but rash in quest of impious gains, shunning the deaths of the dying, and craving the spoils of the dead; forsaking sick wretches lest they by being cured may escape the hand clutching for their estate."[15]

Cyprian denounces the heathen method of dealing with Christians, tearing their bodies, lacerating their vitals, or devising new tortures.[16] Besides in this case tortures, which are used to extort confessions of crime, are not necessary; because Christians readily confess their Christianity. Publicly, openly, in the hearing of your magistrates and governors I freely confess that I am a Christian; why then do you apply tortures to one who thus openly destroys your gods?[17] But as to the main question,

---

[15] Ad. Demet. 10.   [16] Ibid. 12.   [17] Ibid. 13.

Why are these evils permitted? they are the direct judgments of the Almighty.

As to the second question, Why do Christians suffer? Cyprian came to that in his beautiful treatise "On Mortality," written to comfort the Christians in the plague. The first reason is the common humanity which Christians have with others. All the ordinary disabilities of the flesh, all ordinary disasters, must necessarily be common to all who wear the common body.[18] The second reason is the fact that Christians are attacked by the devil more than others.[19] Besides, they must be tried as soldiers, that their courage and constancy may appear. Their trials perfect faith, strengthen virtue.[20] After describing the horrible symptoms of the plague he says: "What grandeur of spirit it is to struggle with all the powers of an unshaken mind against so many onsets of devastation and death! What sublimity to stand erect amid the desolations of the human race and not to lie prostrate with those who have no faith in God! But rather to rejoice, by suffering and showing forth our faith going forward to Christ by the narrow way that Christ trod, we may receive the reward of his life and faith according to His own judgment."[21] As consolation

---

[18] De Mort. 8.   [19] Ibid. 9.   [20] Ibid. 13.   [21] Ibid. 14.

Mercy and Help. 137

Cyprian looks away to the other life—it is Paul's, The sufferings of this present time are not worthy to be compared with the glory that shall be revealed.[22] But there are compensations here: the plague snatches virgins away from the danger of brothels, boys from the perils of their unstable age, and matrons from the torments of the executioner. Besides by all these things the "lukewarm are inflamed, the slack are nerved up, slothful stimulated, deserters compelled to return, heathens constrained to believe, the ancient congregation of the faithful called to rest, the new and abundant congregation of the faithful gathered to battle with a braver vigor to fight without fear of death when the battle shall come."[23]

In addition Cyprian sees in the plague a kind of probation, a testing. This proves its pertinence and necessity. It searches the righteousness of each one; it proves whether the healthy tend the sick, whether relatives love their kindred, masters pity servants, physicians forsake patients, the fierce suppress their violence, rapacious their avarice, the haughty bend their neck, wicked soften their boldness, the rich give. It trains Christians for martyrdom by teaching them not to fear death. "These are

---

[22] Rom. viii, 18.   [23] De Mort. 15.

trainings for us, not deaths. They give the mind the glory of fortitude; by contempt of death they prepare for the crown."[24]

The best part of the treatise is devoted to a beautiful exhortation to fidelity on account of the heavenly rewards that await the faithful. Here Cyprian appears at his best. Why should we bewail those who are "not lost but gone before?"'[25] Why should we wear black here for those who wear white there? Will we lay ourselves open to the reproach of the heathen that the heart does not indorse the testimony of the mouth?[26] Death is the entrance to life. Therefore let us hail the day that calls us home. There our dear ones are waiting for us—parents, brothers, children, all longing for us and solicitous for our salvation. To attain their presence and embrace—what a gladness for them and us. There death can not enter. Then think of the company; the glorious company of the apostles, the host of rejoicing prophets, innumerable multitudes of martyrs,[27] the triumphant virgins, the men of mercy who won the reward of kindness to the poor. To these let us hasten with eager desire; let us crave

---

[24] De Mort. 16. [25] Sciamus non eos amitti sed præmitti. [26] Ibid. 20.
[27] Apostolorum gloriosus chorus;
   Prophetarum exulantium numurus;
   Martyrum innumerabilis populus.

to be quickly with them and come quickly to Christ! May God behold our eager desire; may the Lord Christ look upon this purpose of our mind and faith! He will give the larger rewards of his glory to those whose desires in respect of Himself were greater.[28]

---

[28] De Mort. 26.

CHAPTER XI.

THE LORD'S PRAYER.

THAT the Lord's Prayer was intended as a model and help rather than a form to be strictly followed, is apparent from the fact that Christianity is a religion of the spirit, and from the additional fact that in New Testament times it is never once referred to, and in the post-apostolic writings only in the so-called *Teaching of the Apostles* (viii, 2). Tertullian is the first to treat it (about the close of the second century). In the third or fourth century it entered into the liturgy of the Church, and ever since that has been used by liturgical and many non-liturgical Churches,—by some in the heathen way rebuked by Christ.[1] It speaks highly for Cyprian that in the midst of the anguish of the plague and the care of the Church he could find heart and time to write a treatise on the Lord's Prayer.

Cyprian has a good idea of prayer. After com-

---

[1] Matt. vi, 7.

mending secret prayer, he says that when we come together in one place to "celebrate divine sacrifices with God's priest," we must observe modesty and discipline, not throw abroad our prayers indiscriminately, with loud voices, "nor cast to God with tumultuous wordiness a petition that ought to be commended to God by modesty, for God is the hearer not of the voice, but of the heart,"—a caution that reminds one of the anxious question of a little boy in Pittston, Pa., on hearing the boisterous pleading of some preacher, "Mother, is his God deaf?" God need not be clamorously reminded, says Cyprian, since he sees men's thoughts.[2]

The text of the prayer Cyprian used ran: "Our Father who art in heaven, hallowed be Thy name. Thy kingdom come. Thy will be done, as in heaven so on earth. Give us this day our daily bread. And forgive us our debts as we forgive our debtors. And suffer us not to be led into temptation, but deliver us from evil (or the evil one). Amen."

The first point made is the unselfishness of the prayer. It is not my Father, it is not, my daily bread, but *our* Father, *our* daily bread, *our* debts, lead *us* not, etc. But Cyprian's mind is not so much on the unselfishness of the prayer as on its teaching

---

[2] De Dom. Orat. 4.

of unity. "Our prayer is public and common; when we pray, we pray not for one, but for the whole people, because we, the whole people, are one."[3] Unity is taught everywhere. That is all important.

As to "Father," Cyprian does not see at all any hint of Christ's teaching as to the universal Fatherhood of God. It is only those who believe in Christ, and who in baptism have put Him on, who are God's sons. A sinful people can not be a son, but only those who have received remission of sins and to whom immortality is promised.[4]

"Hallowed be Thy name" means that His name may be hallowed in us by our continual sanctification. This was begun in baptism, which washed us from our sins, but the cleansing must be continued through the grace of God, received in the "name of our Lord Jesus Christ, and by the Spirit of our God."[5]

As to the kingdom ("Thy kingdom come") Cyprian does not have a very clear idea. He apparently makes it equivalent with our rejoicing with Christ hereafter. He says also that Christ himself may be the kingdom of God, "whom we day by day desire to come, whose advent we crave to be quickly manifested to us." As to a progressive ex-

---

[3] De Dom. Orat. 8.   [4] Ibid. 9, 10.   [5] Ibid. 12.

pansion of Christianity until the kingdoms of business, of pleasure, of national affairs, etc., become the kingdoms of Christ, or as to any missionary application of the prayer, Cyprian is silent.[6]

He has excellent remarks on "Thy will be done." He still speaks to us here. The will of God is what Christ taught and did. "Humility in conversation; steadfastness in faith; modesty in words; justice in deeds; mercifulness in works; discipline in morals; to be unable to do a wrong, and to be able to bear a wrong when done; to keep peace with the brethren; to love God with all one's heart; to love Him because He is a Father; to fear Him because He is God; to prefer nothing whatever to Christ because He did not prefer anything to us; to adhere inseparably to His love; to stand by His cross bravely and faithfully; when there is any contest on behalf of his name and honor, to show in words constancy in confession, in torture that confidence wherewith we do battle, in death that patience whereby we are crowned, this is to desire to be fellow-heirs with Christ; this is to do the commandment of God; this is to fulfill the will of the Father."[7] Surely these are golden words. We should also pray for those who are not in the Church, that they "who are as yet in

---

[6] De Dom. Orat. 13.   [7] Ibid. 15.

their first birth of earth, may, being born of water and of the Spirit, begin to be of heaven."

The petition as to our daily bread Cyprian interprets as referring to ordinary food and wealth and to the Eucharist. In the one case we must not long for earthly food, for riches are deceitful and vanishing, besides being a snare to the soul. He takes literally Matt. vi, 34. The Christian is "prohibited from thinking of the morrow; it is a contradiction and a repugnant thing for us to seek to live long in the world since we ask that the kingdom of God should come quickly." The true daily bread is the Eucharistic food of salvation, which we receive daily. This is the body of Christ referred to in John vi, 53, 58. If we remain separate from Christ's body as thus interpreted we can not be saved.[8] Here we have a foundation of monasticism on the one hand and of the highest sacramentarianism on the other.

"Forgive us our debts" makes the spirit of love, the spirit which forgives our enemies, absolutely indispensable to salvation or to the reception of any spiritual grace. No sacrifice is as important as this. Even the blood of martyrdom can not help us here. But Cyprian can not help bringing in even under

---
[8] De Dom. Orat. 18, 19.

this head the great principle of unity. "Our peace and brotherly agreement is a greater sacrifice to God,—and a people united in one in the unity of the Father, and of the Son, and of the Holy Spirit."[9]

Cyprian has a beautiful thought in regard to the petition, "Suffer us not to be led into temptation," when he says that that takes away all boasting. We can not assume anything to ourselves in confession or suffering. "All is attributed to God, and whatever is sought for suppliantly with fear and honor of God, may be granted by His own lovingkindness."[10]

We have the first witness to the Sursum Corda (upward, hearts). When we stand praying, says Cyprian (standing was the usual posture of prayer in the ancient Church, and always on Sunday), we ought to be watchful and earnest with our whole heart, intent on our prayers. The soul must think on nothing but the object of its prayer. "For this reason also the priest, by the way of preface before his prayer, prepares the minds of his brethren by saying: 'Lift up your hearts,' that so upon the people's response, 'We lift them up unto the Lord,' he may be reminded that he himself ought to think of nothing but the Lord."[11]

---

[9] De Dom. Orat. 23. [10] Ibid. 26. [11] Ibid. 31.

Cyprian closes with some excellent rules as to prayer. (1) Be intent on what you ask. (2) Have a background of faithful, holy, and loving living to your prayers. Alms and good deeds are strong backers. (3) Observe regular hours of prayer. Daniel observed the third, sixth, and ninth hour, "as it were for a sacrament of the Trinity, which in the last times had to be manifested."[12] Besides this we must pray in the morning, according to Ps. v, 2, and in the evening, because when the light of day departs we must ask for the advent of Christ, who shall give us the grace of everlasting light. There is no hour excepted for Christians wherein God ought not frequently and always to be worshiped. Day and night, therefore, let us pray.[13]

---

[12] De Dom. Orat. 34, [13] Ibid. 35-6.

CHAPTER XII.

CYPRIAN THE CATHOLIC.

It is not necessary to say that Cyprian—a Christian than whom a more sincere and devoted never lived—held to all those ideas which the Churches Catholic and Protestant have in common. If the Apostles' and Nicene creeds had been presented to him he would have assented to them heartily. All the main facts of Christianity he held to tenaciously. In this chapter an effort will be made to state wherein he differed from evangelical Protestantism, wherein he shows that the world in which he lived in the middle of the third century was a Catholic world.[1] I shall attempt no special logical arrangement in the order of topics.

Few Protestants would find fault with the statement of the nineteenth article of the Church of England. That the "visible Church of Christ is a congregation of faithful men, in which the pure word of

---

[1] I use the word Catholic here as the opposite of Protestant,—those points in which the Roman, Greek, Armenian, and other Eastern Churches agree among themselves, but differ from Protestantism.

God is preached, and the sacraments duly ministered according to Christ's ordinance in all those things that of necessity are requisite to the same." Here the Church is not the clergy, or the bishop, or a company gathered around them, but a collection of believers in Christ who chiefly exalt the word of God, and who in their time and place receive the sacraments. What was Cyprian's view of the Church? It is a company gathered around the bishops, who hold their authority from the apostles, and chiefly from Peter, who received first the commission of authority from Christ, and so is in a sense the foundation or origin of unity. All apostles have equal power with Peter, but since Peter was the first who was designated as the rock, he makes the beginning one and not many. So although there are many bishops who preside in the Church, yet the episcopate is one and undivided, because it is the one chair of Peter.[2] In order to show forth this unity there can necessarily be only one bishop in a place, union with whom is the same as union with Christ. The Church is in the bishop because he is all, and to separate one's self from the bishop is death and hell.[3] "Does any one believe that in one place there can be either many shepherds or many flocks?"[4] Those

---

[2] De Unit. Eccl. 4, 5.   [3] Ibid. 5, 6.   [4] Ibid. 8.

who separate from the Church as thus understood are lost. Their baptisms are spurious, all their apparent Christian acts are of the devil.[5] In fact, they never do thus separate unless they are themselves already apostate. Their separation is on account of a perverse, strife-loving heart.[6] Even if they should give themselves in martyrdom for the Name, it would avail nothing. "He can not be a martyr who is not in the Church."[7]

As to baptism, it is not a sign or seal of grace received by faith, which is the only effective means of salvation, the root of the whole process, but it is itself the gate of salvation. In it we lay aside our earthly birth, are freed from death and the devil, are cleansed from sin, and regenerated. Baptism is the water of salvation and the water of life; by it we live again; it is the resurrection with Christ, the birth of Christians, the heavenly and spiritual birth, the second birth, the new birth. By it we become children of God and are made into the image of God.[8] Nothing could be more Catholic than Cyprian's idea of baptism. With baptism anointing was connected as to-day in Catholic Churches. "It is

---

[5] De Unit. Eccl. 11, 12.   [6] Ibid. 13.   [7] Ibid. 14.
[8] See K. G. Goetz, Das Christentum Cyprians, Giessen, 1896, 62-4, where references to Hartel's edition are given for each of the above statements.

also necessary that he should be anointed who is baptized, so that, having received the chrism, that is, the anointing, he may be anointed of God, and have in him the grace of Christ."[9] This attachment of spiritual grace to material means is thoroughly congenial to the mechanism of Catholicism.

Equally "high" is his view of the Eucharist. It is the "protection of Christ's body and blood, appointed to be a safeguard to the receivers that they may be armed against the adversary with the protection of the Lord's abundance."[10] The Eucharistic bread is the food of salvation, the bread of heaven, prefigured by the manna; the cup makes us oblivious to the old man and the former evil life; it brings back spiritual wisdom; it is the intoxicating healthgiving cup ("the Holy Spirit is not silent concerning the sacrament in the Psalms, making mention of the cup of the Lord and saying, 'Thy best inebriating cup'"). Christ has drunk the saving cup; his blood is wine, for he says, "I am the true vine."[11] Everywhere in Cyprian the Eucharist is a true offering. It is both a priestly self-offering of Christ, and an offering in his memory. As both it is offered in the Church of God and partaken of. The Eucharist is the high priestly

---

[9] Ep. 70 (69), 2.   [10] Ep. 57 (53), 2.   [11] See K. G. Goetz, 67.

CYPRIAN THE CATHOLIC.

memorial offering, the offering of food and drink, which accompanies the bloody offering of Christ, and therefore, as the old high priestly offering of food, is celebrated morning and evening. It is the sacrifice of the new covenant, and it is valid as a sin-offering. The Eucharist is the self-offering of the Lord, not because it is a memorial offering for him on account of his sufferings, but because in the same Christ body and blood are indicated as bread and wine, and in their full meaning are made apparent and figuratively communicated. "And because," says Cyprian, "we make mention of His passion (sufferings and death) in all sacrifice, for it is the passion which we offer as the sacrifice of the Lord; for we ought to do nothing else than He did. For the Scripture says that as often as we offer the cup in commemoration of the Lord and of His passion, we do the same that it is evident the Lord did."[13] It would be too much too say that Cyprian had the fully developed sacrificial conception of the Eucharist common to later Catholicism, but he was a good way on the road, and he would be perfectly at home in the idea, if not in the method, of a High

---

[13] Hartel, 714. See K. G. Goetz, 87, whose thorough exposition of Cyprian's views is objective and reliable, though his divisional terminology is whimsical, and calls forth the well-deserved rebuke of Lüdemann in Theol. Jahresb. 16 (1896), 163.

Church celebration. So the minister, or rather the bishop, is always a priest with him.

An interesting question is that concerning the Churchly forgiveness granted to the penitent lapsed. Was this an act simply of earthly local jurisdiction, such as the taking back of a sinner in a Protestant Church, a recognition by the Church of what might be charitably assumed to have taken place between the sinner and God, or was it a real judicial communication in the name of Christ and in His earthly place of forgiveness and peace? In other words, was Catholic absolution as early as Cyprian? On one side of the question is Karl Goetz, on the other side is Karl Müller.[14] The former has given us an exceedingly valuable pamphlet, but I can not but think that Müller is nearer the mind of Cyprian. With Cyprian the Church is a divine institution in the fullest sense. What she, through her bishops, in communion with her presbyters, binds or looses on earth is bound or loosed in heaven. The Church is the bride of God, His house, His temple. To belong to her, to be at peace with her, is essential to the hope of salvation. These principles led Cyprian to

---

[14] Goetz (to be distinguished from K. G. Goetz), Die Busslehre Cyprians, Königsb. in Pr., 1895; Müller, " Die Bussinstitution in Karthago unter Cyprian," 3d part, in Zeitschrift f. Kirchengeschichte, Oct. 1895 (xvi), 187 ff.

Cyprian the Catholic.

be more and more lenient with the lapsed, in regard to their return to the Church, as we have seen. In some way the Church must try to get them back before they die. Peace with her is necessary, if they would have peace with God. Her absolution of the penitent holds before God. Of course, this is only in the case God has Himself forgiven the penitent, and to assure the Church of that the martyrs' testimonies come in. The rôle of martyrs has already been described. Their part in this feature of Church life has passed away; but in all Catholic Churches it still remains true—whatever differences in detail or in form may be seen in granting the absolution—that the Church as the indispensable vehicle of salvation hands out to the penitent the certificate of peace, without which (except to those debarred without their fault) salvation is impossible. This is the eternal note of Catholicism, and it goes straight back to Cyprian. The Catholic Church did well to canonize him.[15] The wholesale remission by martyrs or confessors Cyprian repudiated;[16] but when the full amount of penitential works was accomplished, then remission by mar-

---

[15] " I remit everything. . . . I almost sin myself in remitting sins more than I ought." (Ep. 59 (54), 16.) The sinner must confess his sins in this world, "while the satisfaction and remission made by the priests are pleasing to the Lord." (De Lapsis, 29.)   [16] De Lapsis, 18.

tyrs or bishops was entirely valid. In fact, it was necessary if the lapsed should be saved.[17]

Müller calls attention to the fact that all along it had been recognized that those endowed with the Spirit could forgive sin.[18] What Cyprian did was to expand this to include the bishops as the divinely appointed heads of the Church, through whom the Spirit spake as really as through the Spirit-gifted of old. Nor was it new with Cyprian that outside of the Church there is no salvation; what was new was his definition of unity as centered in his kind of bishops. Even the martyr outside of Cyprian's kind of unity is lost.[19] Of course, no more than in the Catholic Church to-day does membership in itself guarantee salvation, but with Cyprian the earthly and heavenly Church coincided thus far that all penitents forgiven by the former were received by the latter, and only those. Cyprian never dreamed of that modern gloss invented by Jesuit and other theologians, that one might belong to the soul of the Church without actual membership in the body itself, and thus make a loophole for Protestants. With him no piety or good works outside of unity avail. He, like the older Roman Catholics, would have consigned all Protestants to hell without a

[17] Ep. 57 (53). 1. [18] Z. K-G., 16, 199. [19] Ep. 55 (51): 17, 29.

moment's hesitation. The moderns in this respect are better Christians, but worse Catholics.

It is not meant, of course, that the Roman Catholic paraphernalia of forgiveness was installed as early as Cyprian. That came after a long development. But the substance was there. The penitent sinner the Church forgave through her bishops, and what she loosed was loosed above.

In regard to merit also Cyprian was Catholic. He had a well defined plan of salvation which he sketches in his book "Of Works and Alms." First, there is the atonement of Christ. "The Father sent the Son to preserve us and give us life; the Son was willing to be sent and to become the Son of man that He might make us sons of God; humbled Himself that He might raise up the people who before were apostate; was wounded that He might heal our wounds; served that He might draw out to liberty those who were in bondage; and died that he might set forth immortality to mortals.[20] Then, there is baptism which through the "blood and sanctification of Christ" washes away the stains of venial sin, and in the case of adults (penitence and faith in Christ being assumed) all the sins committed before baptism. Now what about sins committed af-

---

[20] De Op. et Eleem. 1.

ter baptism? Cyprian sees through the whole process with a lawyer's clearness. What would we do, he says, considering our weakness and human frailty, "unless the Divine mercy coming once more to our aid, should open some way of securing salvation by pointing out works of justice and mercy, so that by almsgiving we may wash away whatever foulness we subsequently contract."[21] He quotes Prov. xvi, 6, "By almsgiving and faith sins are purged,"[22] and Ecclesiasticus iii, 3, "As water extinguisheth fire, so almsgiving quencheth sin," and attributes both passages to the Holy Spirit. "Here also," he adds, "it is shown and proved, that as in the laver of saving water the fire of Gehenna is extinguished, so by almsgiving and work of righteousness the flames of sin are subdued. And because in baptism remission of sins is granted once for all, constant and ceaseless labor, following the likeness of baptism, once more bestows the mercy of God."[23] Then by misquotation and misunderstanding of Luke xi, 41, he makes Christ responsible for this same teaching; after we have become foul after baptism, Christ teaches (Cyprian says) that by alms we may become clean.[24]

---

[21] De Op. et Eleem. 1.   [22] Septuagint.   [23] De Op. et Eleem. 2.
[24] For the interpretation of Luke xi, 41, see Meyer ad loc; and Grimm, N. T. Lex. Ed. Thayer, s. ἔνειμι. Perhaps better still: things within the soul; that is, see that ye have soul qualities out of which ye can

Cyprian is thoroughly committed to a work-holiness Christianity. This is partly due to his taking the Old Testament Apocrypha as law and gospel. If he had studied Paul more and Tobit less he might have reached different results. The "wholesome remedy which God has provided for the curing of our wounds anew"[25] is alms. In fact, by these God is propitiated. "By works of righteousness God is satisfied, and with the deserts of mercy sins are cleansed."[26] "Prayer is good, with fasting and alms; because alms doth deliver from death, it purgeth away sins."[27] This passage, says Cyprian, shows that our petitions become efficacious by almsgiving, that life is redeemed from dangers by almsgiving, that souls are delivered from death by almsgiving.[28]

The commercialism inherent in all forms of Catholicism comes out plainly in Ep. 76, 1, where the reward to the martyrs in the mines is graduated exactly according to their hardship and tortures—"advancing by the tediousness of their tortures to more ample titles of merits, to receive as many payments (*tot mercedes*) in heavenly rewards as days counted in punishments." He has in view the "merit of religion and faith," so that they shall re-

---

[25] De Op. et Eleem. 3.   [26] Ibid. 5.   [27] Tob. 12: 8, 9.
[28] De Op. et El. 5.

ceive from the Lord, the "crown of their merits," by which the divine esteem (*divina dignatio*) has honored them.[29]

We get the same thing in the offerings of the Lord's Supper. Harnack says that Cyprian has advanced the idea of offering or sacrifice in the cultus of the Church in three ways: 1. He assigned to a specific priesthood a specific offering, viz., the offering at the Lord's Supper. 2. He has designated the passion of the Lord, even the blood of Christ and the Lord's host (*dominica hostia*) as the subject or object of Eucharistic offering. 3. He has definitely placed the celebration of the Lord's Supper under the point of view of the incorporation of the congregation and its single members in Christ, and was the first to witness in a distinct way that to the commemoration of those who make the offering (the living and the dead) a special significance is to be ascribed; though this is nothing but a strengthened petition.[30] "In the sacrifices," says Cyprian, "I offer prayer with many, remembering you," etc.[31] The Numidian captives were to present the names of the donors to their release in the sacrifices and prayers,[32] where sacrifice means the Eucharistic of-

---

[29] Dignatio is mistranslated by Wallis "condescension." It is a recognition of worth, esteem founded on merit. [30] Dogmengeschichte 3. Aufl. I, 428 f; Eng. tr. II, 136–7. [31] Ep. 37 (15), 1. [32] Ibid. 62 (59), 4.

fering. This offering could go to the credit of the dead as well as of the living.[33] We must not think of this as the full-fledged Catholic purgatory and prayers for the release of souls therefrom, for there was no doubt that the martyrs at least were in the full felicity of Christ; but it was the beginning of it. The Eucharistic offering availed for much. A man offers for his dead wife on the anniversary of her home-going in order, says Tertullian, "to help along her eternal quickening and her participation in the first resurrection." "It is the beginning of a custom which afterwards was built up into the doctrine of purgatory, which was the chief lever for charity in the Middle Ages, yes, the central point around which it revolves. From a thank-offering the Eucharistic oblation becomes a work directed to the obtaining of grace."[34]

It seems also that in Cyprian we have the rudiments of the doctrine of the treasury of merits laid up with God, out of which help can come to those in need.[35] He says that the perogatives of the martyrs are able to help before God those who have re-

---

[33] For the living see 17 (11), 2; for the dead 39 (33), 3; 12 (36), 2.

[34] Uhlhorn, Christliche Liebesthätigkeit in der alten Kirche, 2. Aufl., Stuttg. 1882, 138.

[35] This is the opinion of Wirth in his able and exhaustive Der Verdienst-Begriff in der christlichen Kirche, II, Der Verdienst-Begriff bei Cyprian. Leipz. 1901. See pp. 89 f., 138 ff., 143 f.

ceived from them letters of peace,[36]—help them even with regard to their sins.[37] In extending favor to returning sinners God can have regard to what martyrs have asked for them or priests have done.[38] Martyrs have merits more than sufficient for themselves. Their martyrdom admits them to glory, so that all their other holiness, heroism, merits, fidelity, etc., is superfluous, so far as being necessary for them alone. It therefore goes to help others for whom they pray. This help will especially accrue at the Day of Judgment. We believe, he says, that the merits of martyrs and the works of the righteous are of great avail with the Judge; but that will be when the Day of Judgment shall come, when at the end of the world His people shall stand before the tribunal of Christ.[39]

These intercessions the saints departed also offer, If any of us shall go hence the first, our love may continue in the presence of the Lord, and our prayers for our brethren and sisters not cease in the presence of the Father's mercy.[40] O remember us, he asks the virgins, when virginity shall begin to be rewarded in you.[41]

This whole Catholic doctrine of merit as founded

---

[36] Ep. 18 (12), 1. [37] Ibid. 19 (13), 2. [38] De Lapsis, 36.
[39] Ibid. 17, Cf. Peters, Cyprian von Karthago, 154–5.
[40] Ep. 60 (56), 5. [41] De Habitu Virg. 24.

CYPRIAN THE CATHOLIC. 161

by Tertullian and Cyprian is as false as it is plausible. We all owe to God a perfect service; none of us has rendered it. What we are we have received, and what we have done we have done through God's grace. God rewards our good works, but this very reward is of grace. The holiest martyr has done only his duty, and if that should be put over against his sins, which would weigh the heavier? Good works are among the indispensable conditions of salvation for those who have opportunity to do them, because they are the fruit of love, which is the fruit and test of faith. But the philosophy of Christianity is in the familiar lines:

> "Nothing in my hands I bring,
> Simply to Thy cross I cling." [42]

Cyprian also laid the foundation of monasticism. The monastic spirit breathes all through his treatise "On the Dress of Virgins." All who are baptized have put off the old man in the saving laver, and have been renewed by the Spirit in a second nativity; but the greater holiness and truth of that repeated birth belongs to you (virgins) who have no longer any desires of the flesh and of the body.

---

[42] See also Wirth, lib. cit. 145ff, and the literature he refers to in the notes.

Only the things which belong to virtue and the Spirit have remained in you to glory.[43] There is the lower life for ordinary Christians, and the higher for those who crucify the flesh. He tells the lapsed that such sins as theirs require extraordinary severities. They must wear out their nights in watchings and wailings, occupy all their time in lamentation, lie on the ground, cling close to the ashes, and be surrounded with sackcloth and filth. "After losing the raiment of Christ you must be willing now to have no clothing; after the devil's meat you must prefer fasting; be earnest in righteous works whereby sins may be purged; frequently apply yourself to almsgiving whereby souls are freed from death. . . . Let all your estate be laid out for the healing of your wound."[44] Virginity, almsgiving, poverty, coarseness and scantiness of clothing, despisal of the world,—all these are specially meritorious before God.[45] All the roots of monasticism are in Cyprian. To live ascetically, says Pontius, was his highest ideal.[46]

---

[43] De Hab. Virg. 23.　　[44] De Lapsis, 35.
[45] See Wirth, 65, with notes.　　[46] Vita Cypriani, 2. See Böhringer, 835.

CHAPTER XIII.

WAS CYPRIAN A ROMAN CATHOLIC?

WE must not suppose that Cyprian's Catholicism was that of later times. Ever and anon Christian sentiments burst forth, and principles both in doctrine and life thoroughly in accordance with the Gospel. For it is written, he says, that the just shall live by faith. If ye are just and live by faith, if you truly believe in Christ, why, since you are about to be with Christ, and die secure of the Lord's promise, do you not embrace the assurance that ye are called to Christ, rejoice that ye are freed from the devil?[1] Though such passages are rare, though Cyprian looks upon justification in a thoroughly legal way, as Wirth has abundantly shown in his section on his use of justificare, justus, justitia,[2] though the idea of merit is hardly absent in any of these passages, yet it was the Catholicism of the middle of the third century (not even of the fourth) which Cyprian represents. There is no purgatory

---

[1] De Mortal. 3. [2] Wirth, 128 ff.

in his writings, though there is, as we have seen, the helpful intercession of saints here and hereafter. God's people depart immediately at death to the celestial land to be with Christ. This is the undertone everywhere of his book on "Mortality." This does not mean that the dead could not be benefited by the prayers and eucharistic commemorations of the living, for such commemorations were well established in Cyprian's time. "We always offer sacrifices for them, as you remember, as often as we celebrate the passions and days of the martyrs in the annual commemoration."[3] A man had appointed a clergyman executor to his estate, contrary to the action of some council, and Cyprian, with his high priestly views, thought that these secular duties, which ministers then and long afterwards performed, interfered with their calling, and he therefore advises that "no offering shall be made to him, nor any sacrifice be celebrated for his repose." No prayer shall be made in the Church for him.[4] It therefore appears that, though the offerings for the martyrs were in the nature of commemorative thanksgivings and not to alleviate their lot (for they went immediately into full felicity), yet it was believed that for others prayers and sacrifices

---

[3] Ep. 39 (33), 3. See also 12 (36), 2.   [4] Ibid. 1 (65), 2.

Was Cyprian a Roman Catholic? 165

could conduce to their repose,—where we have the germs of the mediæval purgatory, indulgencies, etc.

There is no mariolatry in Cyprian. If Mary's name is ever mentioned, it is only casually.

The chief question is Cyprian's relation to the see of Rome. Did he acknowledge the bishop of Rome as supreme pontiff of the Church, whose authority as a ruler and infallibility as a teacher must be respected at all hazards? We have already seen that Cyprian's conception of the Church was that of an organization grouped around the bishops. The bishop was the center of the Church, and each bishop was co-ordinate with every other. Their united decision in council was binding on the province which they represented, though in matters of conscience each bishop could take his own line, so long as he remained in external unity with his brethren. There could only be one canonically elected bishop in a town. If another is elected he is by that very fact outside of the Church, outside of salvation, outside of the covenanted mercies of God. "They are a Church, who are a people united to a priest, and the flock which adheres to its pastor. Whence you ought to know that the bishop is in the Church, and the Church in the bishop; and if any one be not with the bishop, he is not in the Church.

The Church which is catholic and one is not cut nor divided, but is indeed connected and bound together by the cement of priests who cohere with one another."[5] "There is one God," he says, "and one Christ, one altar, one priesthood, and one chair founded upon the rock of the word of the Lord."[6] That was the chair of Peter upon which the Church was to be built. Now the question is: Is that chair the see of Rome to which all must be obedient, from which all must receive law, or is it the episcopate which traces its descent back to the apostles,[7] and especially to Peter as the first in time to whom Christ granted authority in the Church? Or if agreement with the chair of Peter (Rome) is necessary, is it only when that chair remains in union with the Christian tradition and the universal episcopate? In the last analysis, who rules the Church, the episcopate or the Roman bishop?

The bishops demand and weigh the evidence of the election and fitness of Cornelius as Bishop of Rome, and only after that do they acknowledge him. They labor to maintain the unity delivered by the Lord through His apostles and to us, his successors, and it is ours to gather in the wandering sheep,[8]—

---

[5] Ep. 66 (68), 8. **Priest and priesthood generally mean bishop and episcopate with Cyprian.** [6] Ibid. 43 (39), 5.

[7] "Christ says to the apostles, and thereby to all chief rulers who by vicarious ordination succeed to the apostles," 66 (68), 4. [8] 45 (41), 3.

Was Cyprian a Roman Catholic? 167

a passage which makes the episcopate the guardians of unity. The bishop of Rome, however, is part of that unity, and they therefore feel it necessary to support him,[9] him who occupies the place of Peter and the grade or degree (gradus) of the sacerdotal chair.[10] Rome is the chair of Peter and the chief (principalis) Church, whence sacerdotal unity takes its rise,[11]—one of those delightful complimentary expressions which may mean much or little, and whose meaning must after all be interpreted by the whole life history of the man who used it, and who evidently did not place all the weight on it a later Roman would, for in this very letter he denounces those who carry appeals from Africa to Rome, as though (he says sarcastically) the authority of the bishops in Africa seems too little. But even Peter, says Cyprian, whom first (*primum*) the Lord chose, and upon whom He built His Church, when Paul disputed with him concerning circumcision, did not claim anything to himself insolently, nor arrogantly assume anything so as to say that he held the primacy, or that he ought to be obeyed by novices and those lately come,[12]—from which it is apparent that, although in Cyprian's mind Peter had a certain

---

[9] Ep. 48 (44), 3. [10] Ep. 55 (51), 8. [11] Ep. 59 (54), 14.
[12] Ep. 71 (70), 3.

primacy (not necessarily the same as supremacy), it did not show itself either in the rightness of his opinions or in his insisting on them.

Another interesting passage seems to confirm the impression already received that Peter's primacy was due to simple priority in time, that thus he was the source of unity, but that in all substantial respects other apostles were fully equal to him. He is speaking of the power of remitting sins in baptism. He says that "first of all the Lord gave that power to Peter, upon whom He built the Church, and whence he appointed the source of unity—the power, namely, that whatsoever he loosed on earth should be loosed in heaven. After the resurrection He speaks to the apostles, saying (here he quotes John xx, 21-23). Whence we perceive, says Cyprian, that all those who are set over the Church and established in the Gospel law, are allowed to baptize and to give remission of sins (not those outside). Here the primacy of all the apostles is made co-ordinate in spiritual functions with the prior chronological primacy of Peter.[13] The token or source of unity is Peter, because to him alone the charge was first given; but the powers

---

[13] Ep. 73 (72), 7. The same thought is in Firmilian to Cyprian, 75 (74), 16.

Was Cyprian a Roman Catholic? 169

thus given were subsequently shared by all absolutely alike. That is Cyprian's thought.

More interesting still is the inference of Firmilian, who echoes Cyprian, that the Roman bishop is only in the succession of Peter when he is true to Peter's doctrine. He is denouncing Stephen, the bishop of Rome, for advocating the efficacy of baptism by heretics. "Nor does he (Stephen) understand that the truth of the Christian rock is overshadowed and in some measure abolished by him when he thus betrays or deserts unity."[14]

Nor does it appear that this general result is affected by the famous passage in his early book (251), the "De Unitate Ecclesiæ," even with the alleged interpolations (in italics), which I now cite:

The Lord said unto Peter (here follows Matt. xvi, 18, 19). *And to the same He says after His resurrection, Feed My sheep.* He builds *His* Church upon *that* one *and to him intrusts His sheep to be fed.* And although after His resurrection He assigns equal power to all His apostles and says (cites John xx, 21-23). Nevertheless in order to make the unity manifest He *established one chair, and* by His own authority appointed origin of the same unity beginning from one. Certainly the rest

---

[14] Ep. 75 (74), 17.

of the apostles were that which Peter also was, endued with equal partnership both of honor and office, but the beginning sets out from unity, *and primacy is given to Peter that one Church of Christ and one chair may be pointed out; that all are apostles, and one flock is shown to be fed by all the apostles with one-hearted accord*—that one Church of Christ may be pointed out. It is this Church which the Holy Spirit in the person of the Lord speaks of in the Song of Songs, saying: "My dove is one, My perfect one, one is she to her mother, elect to her who brought her forth." He who holds not this unity of the Church, does he believe that he holds the faith? He who strives and rebels against the Church, *he who deserts the chair of Peter on which the Church is founded*, does he trust that he is in the Church?[15]

Here we have the Cyprianic principles of unity just as in his Epistles. (1.) Unity springs from Peter, because he was the beginning of these grants of power from Christ. We must hold, therefore, with him. (2.) Exactly the same power was given to all the apostles, who derive this, not from Peter, but from Christ. But in true-hearted accord they stand in with Peter, whose chair is the beginning

---

[15] De Unit. Eccl. 4. For full textual apparatus see Benson, 549-52.

Was Cyprian a Roman Catholic?

and symbol of unity. Nothing is said here about the authority and the infallibility of the bishops of Rome, whether those bishops might not err, or if they did what should be the proper attitude toward them. If the italicized words are really interpolated, would they not have stated the Roman claims more explicitly, would they not have echoed later controversies, would they have simply been content to round out the passage to bring it into harmony with later utterances of Cyprian? It is by no means true that Cyprian is represented here as teaching the cardinal doctrine of the Roman see.[16] It is *a* cardinal teaching, but it is not her special doctrine. Protestants believe that the Church was founded upon Peter in a special sense, historically shown by his work with the Jews in Acts ii and with the Gentiles in Acts x. They believe it is necessary to hold with him in order to be in the unity of the Church, and they believe firmly that if the chief pastors in Rome had always remained true to him, union with them would also be in a sense a symbol and test of unity. There is nothing specially Roman in the full text, interpolated or not, in the *Unity of the Church*.

The real questions are: Did Cyprian hold that

---

[16] Benson is wrong here, 203.

the bishop of Rome had in himself plenary authority in the Church? That he was an infallible teacher? That all bishops are under him and hold from him? In other words, did the fact that Peter was the beginning and foundation of unity guarantee the later claims for those who were supposed to sit on his seat? Two or three facts from Cyprian's life will answer these questions.

Two Spanish bishops, Basilides, of Leon, and Martial, of Merida, had received certificates of idolatry, and thus according to the custom of the Church had debarred themselves for life from office. Basilides had also blasphemed Christ in sickness, and Martial had joined a pagan guild or college with its heathen rites, and had two of his children buried with these rites. They subsequently repented, went to Rome, and apparently received assurances from Stephen, the new bishop there, that he would still regard them as bishops. Cyprian apologizes for Stephen on account of distance and ignorance ("went to Rome and deceived Stephen our colleague, placed at a distance, and ignorant of what had been done, and of the truth, to canvass that he [Basilides] might be replaced unjustly in the episcopate"). This created a new situation. Who were the real bishops of Leon and Merida—the deposed bishops, bishops recognized still by Stephen, or their successors, lawfully elected and dedicated? For advice as to this the Churches themselves appeal not to Stephen, but to Cyprian and his African brethren. A council is held at Carthage, 254 (the Fourth Cyprianiac Council), and the result is given in Cyprian's letter 67.

This is a most interesting letter. It gives Cyprian's answer to the question, Does grave sin invalidate ministerial acts? He answers with an emphatic Yes—buttressed as usual with Old Testament passages like Ex. xix, 22; xxviii, 43. And all who can unite with such a priest share in his defilement. The letter also shows that the laymen of the local Churches must be present at the election of a bishop, not, it would appear, formally to elect by casting votes, but to investigate as to character of the nominee and to signify to the bishops present as to his fitness,—the final decision being with the clergy and bishops present, but never without the presence and co-operation of the laymen. Sometimes the laymen, as we have seen, played the controlling rôle. The neighboring bishops laid on hands in consecration. But the significance of the letter here is that Stephen's part in this Spanish business is brushed aside as of no account whatever, and decision given according to the well-known Cyprianic principles, as though there were no Roman bishop in the world.[17]

Marcian, bishop of Arles in France, had joined the Novatians so far as not to admit the lapsed, however penitent and desirous. As this in Cyprian's opinion endangered their souls, he was much exercised over it. A bishop of Lyons had called his attention to it. If the neighboring bishops would not do their duty in electing a successor to Marcian, it was the bishop of Rome's duty, as the bishop of the nearest so-called apostolic see and of the greatest Church of the West, to urge them to do it. But Stephen was apparently unconcerned. Therefore Cyprian writes him, calling his attention to the moral responsibility of all the bishops of the universal flock, and urging him to write to the laymen of the Arles Church to the effect that Marcian be excommunicated and another substituted. He is also asked to write to the bishops of the province

---

[17] Ep. 67. Peters (Cyprian von Karthago, 483) is in error in saying that on the return of Basilides from Rome most of the Spanish bishops changed their attitude toward him and Martial, and acknowledged them as brothers in office. All that Cyprian says is that "some among our colleagues rashly hold communion with Basilides" (67, 9), though whether Stephen's action had anything to do with it we do not know. Peters also says (p. 486) that Cyprian is not giving a judgment, but an opinion. But the utmost decision and positiveness rings through the letter; there is not the least consciousness of a revision of its judgment being possible.

to see to it that Marcian no longer "insults an assembly." It does not appear that Stephen's action would be different from that of any other prominent bishop in urging discipline on neighboring Churches. Cyprian's whole letter, with its freedom of address and consciousness of equality, does not bespeak the papacy in the historic sense.[18] The remark of Peters that Cyprian here acknowledges Stephen's ordinance and immediate jurisdiction over the whole Church is so nearly made out of whole cloth that it may be taken as a type of such statements made by Roman partisan historians.[19]

The most famous case, however, is the quarrel with Stephen over the baptismal question, and that deserves a separate chapter.

---

[18] Ep. 68 (66).

[19] Peters, 479. My judgment of this whole aspect of Cyprian's Catholicism is borne out by K. G. Goetz, who says that for Cyprian the "basis of the Church is an intellectual legal conception which expresses itself in the political institution of the episcopate as a college, as a body (corpus), not of the Roman episcopate alone." He says that the fact that Cyprian designates the universal episcopate as a college (collegium) shows that he ascribes to all the bishops equal power and equal right (Recht), and he quotes Mommsen (Abriss d. röm. Staatsrecht, 120) as saying that the "fact of being in a college (Collegialität) demands the equality in rights of the officers in the college, therefore the equal title and equal authority in office." See Goetz, Das Christentum Cyprians, 128, and note. Substantially the same view comes out in the thorough study of a Roman Catholic scholar, J. Delarochelle, L'idée de l'église dans St. Cyprien, in Etudes d'Hist. et deLittér. relig. 1896, No. 1, 519-33. Though the Roman bishop was the official representative of unity, all bishops were equal in power and honor. He says that Cyprian's conception of the Church was an imperfect one, and did not comport with the fact of the Roman primacy.

CHAPTER XIV.

THE GREAT CONTROVERSY WITH ROME.

It was the universal belief in the third century that baptism washed away the stain of original sin, made the baptized a child of God, and thus brought him into the family of the redeemed. Along with this was the idea of the Church as the ark of salvation, outside of which all were swept away by the devouring floods. Now as soon as movements arose which the larger Church disowned, or forced out into separate existence, the question arose, What about the baptism administered by those outside, either by those heretical, or schismatic, or both? Does their baptism give life, does it incorporate into Christ, does their repetition of the Name give the blessing of the Name? If so baptism need not be repeated; if not, all baptized by heretics or schismatics must be baptized again, their former baptism not being a real baptism at all. On the one side of this question stood Cyprian, on the other, Stephen, bishop of Rome.

It must be confessed that Cyprian had the better tradition, so far as testimonies attest it. Clement of Alexandria called baptism by heretics no proper and genuine baptism.[1] Tertullian energetically protested on the same side. Heretics have nothing common with the Church, not the same God, nor the same Christ, and therefore not the same baptism, and therefore one can not receive baptism from them.[2] In the latter half of the second century, the Montanists of Asia Minor, who agreed with the Church on all essential matters of doctrine, precipitated a discussion of the subject, and at synods held at Iconium and at Synnada, baptism outside of the Church was rejected.[3] "Heretics can neither baptize nor do anything holy and with the Spirit because they are foreign to spiritual and divine sanctity."[4] Hippolytus says that Callistus was the first to introduce a repetition of baptism in Rome.[5]

We do not know how the controversy begun. The first document seems to be a letter of Cyprian to Magnus, A. D. 205, in answer to a question whether the Novatianists in returning to the so-

---

[1] Strom. 1, 19.
[2] De Bapt. 15, written in premontanist period, says Bonwetsch, against Benson, 338. See the admirable article by Bonwetsch, Ketzertaufe und Streit darüber, in Hauck–Herzog, Realencyk. f. protest. Theol. u. Kirche, (1901), 270–5.   [3] Eusebius H. E. 7: 7, 5. Firmilian in Cypr. Ep. 75 (74), 7.
[4] Firmilian, as in rote 3.   [5] Philos. 9, 7.

called Catholic Church should be rebaptized. Cyprian answers with his usual decision and peremptoriness. He never balks at the fact that Novatian held the Catholic faith; the mere fact that he is outside of what he (Cyprian) calls the Catholic Church decided the issue. He has departed from "charity and the unity of the Catholic Church," and on the ground of Matt. xviii, 17, he is worse than a heathen and a publican, because he has "forged false altars, lawless priesthoods and sacrilegious sacrifices, and has corrupted names." The Church is one, baptism is one, and baptism is in the Church only, according to Eph. v, 26; how then can any one outside be cleansed with the saving laver? If any one says that they hold the same Trinity and the same interrogatory in baptizing as the Church—and Cyprian quotes the interrogatory, Dost thou believe the remission of sins and life eternal through the holy Church?—then the answer is, They lie, since they have not the Church. Cyprian refers to the history of Korah, Dathan, and Abiram, who knew the same God as Moses, yet because they set up in opposition to Aaron, they were punished for their irreligious and lawless endeavors. All who joined with them were punished also, as it shall be also with the schismatics and all who follow them. How can those without the Holy Ghost confer the Holy Ghost, as baptism does? Baptism is the remission of sins, and it is therefore necessary that those who baptize should have the Holy Ghost. But by the fact that it is the universal custom of the Church in receiving those baptized without to lay hands on them that they may receive the Holy Ghost, it is confessed that they have not the Spirit. It is certain, therefore, that those thus baptized have not received the remission of sins. To receive this, then, they must be baptized with the baptism of the Church, where only remission of sins may be had.[6]

False and arbitrary exegesis was not wanting.

---

[6] Ep. 69 (75). This epistle closes (12-16) with an answer to the question whether those who have been sprinkled on a sick-bed are sanctified (so-called clinic baptism). While Cyprian distinguishes this from the regular "washing of salvation," from "ecclesiastical baptism," which at this time was always by immersion, he says it is valid and need not be supplemented by ordinary baptism. If the clinics have had faith, if their subsequent life shows the reality of their faith, they received the full mercy of God. Nothing need be added. For (1) washing of sins is a different matter from the washing of the body, where water and saltpeter and the other appliances are needed. "In another way is the heart of the believer washed; in another way is the mind of man purified by the merit of faith." (2) Sprinkling was recognized by God as a symbol of cleansing, according to Ezek. xxxvi, 25-6; Num. viii, 5-7; xix, 8-13. Hence sprinkling of water "avails equally with the washing of salvation; and when this is done in the Church (that is, in the society, or in communion with the Church), where the faith both of the giver and the receiver is sound, all things hold, and may be consummated perfectly by the majesty of the Lord and by the truth of faith." (3) Facts show that those "baptized by urgent necessity in sickness, and obtain grace, are free from the unclean spirit, and live in the Church in praise and honor," which is a proof that they have received the Spirit.

"They have forsaken Me, the fountain of living waters, and have hewed out broken cisterns which can hold no water,"[7] refers to the schismatics. Of their baptism the warning applies, "Keep thee from strange water, and drink not from the fountain of strange water."[8] John's prophecy of antichrists refers to them.[9] Can these give the grace of Christ?

The water used in baptism must first be cleansed and sanctified by the priest. But how can a schismatic priest cleanse when he himself is unclean. "Whatsoever the unclean person toucheth shall be unclean."[10] Besides, every baptized person is also anointed with oil so that he may be anointed of God, and have in him the grace of Christ. But the oil is sanctified on the altar, where the Eucharist is offered; but how can a heretic or schismatic do that when he has neither the Church nor the altar? See, too, what the Holy Spirit says in the Psalms: "Let not the oil of the sinner anoint my head."[11] Again what prayer can a priest who is impious or a sinner offer for a baptized person? Since it is written, "God heareth not a sinner, but if any man be a worshiper of God, and doeth His will, him He heareth."[12] With such relentless logic, built on such perverted Scripture, did the good bishop condemn

---

[7] Jer. ii, 13. [8] Prov. ix, 19 (LXX). [9] 1 John ii, 18, 19.
[10] Num. xix, 2. [11] Ps. cxli, 15 (LXX). [12] John ix, 31.

the baptism of all outside his episcopal unity as sacrilegious, and their persons as utterly lost to the grace and mercy of God.[13] "He that is baptized by one dead, what availeth his washing?"[14]

What were the arguments of Stephen? Unfortunately we have not an epistle of his extant. All we can do is to get a glimpse here and there of the contrary arguments from the correspondence of Cyprian. First, "they say they follow ancient custom."[15] Cyprian explains this by the fact that the first heretics had previously been baptized in the Church, and, of course, when they returned it was not necessary to rebaptize them. Besides, he says, no custom can stand against reason. Again it is said: He who is baptized might receive remission of sins according to what he believed.[16] Cyprian replies to this that no one can have true faith outside of the Church. Either they are manifestly heretical like Marcion and other heretics, or they are perfidious, blasphemous, and contentious, which makes their faith no faith. Some quoted Phil. i, 18, but that refers to envious brethren within the Church, not to baptism by those outside.[17] Others say: All who are baptized anywhere and anyhow in

---

[13] Ep. 70 (69). [14] Ecclus. xxxiv, 25, (Ep. 71 (70), 1).
[15] Ep. 71 (70), 2. [16] Ep. 73 (72), 4. [17] Ibid. § 14.

the name of Christ have obtained the grace of baptism.[18] Not so, replies Cyprian, for not every one that says, Lord, Lord, shall enter the kingdom of heaven. Only those things which are done in the truth of Christ are accepted by Him. It is said that this non-acknowledgment will debar heretics from coming back. Not at all; it will have just the contrary effect. Why should he come back if he has true baptism? Having that, they will think they have everything. But when they know that no remission of sins can be given outside of the Church, they will eagerly hasten back to us.[19]

The two chief points of Stephen were tradition and the majesty of the Name. While Cyprian will not acknowledge that there is any true tradition on Stephen's side, he makes a powerful plea against tradition dominating truth.[20] One can almost hear the strains of the old Protestants controverting Rome. "What obstinacy, what presumption to prefer human tradition to Divine ordinance, and not to observe that God is angry when tradition relaxes or passes by the divine precepts, as he says by Isaiah, 'This people honoreth Me with their lips, but their heart is far from Me. In vain do they

---

[18] Ep. 73 (72), 16 ff. In these sections of this great epistle Cyprian argues cogently against the validity of baptism by Gnostic Christians.
[19] Ep. 73 (72), 24.   [20] Ep. 74 (73). 2-4, 9.

worship me, teaching the doctrines and commandments of men.'" "Nor ought custom, which had crept in among some, prevent the truth from conquering, for custom without truth is the old age of error."

As to the Name availing, they really confess that it does not avail, because they (Stephen and his party) always lay their hands on the returning heretic that he may receive the Holy Spirit. But by allowing his baptism they allow that in a real sense he has already received the Holy Ghost. He has been sanctified, his sins have been washed away, he has put on Christ, and can Christ be put on without the Spirit, or the Spirit be separated from Christ? Water alone is not able to sanctify, unless a man has also the Holy Spirit. Later he receives the Holy Spirit in fuller measure in the anointing and imposition of hands, but this would be impossible if he had not already been born by baptism into the Holy Spirit.[21]

As to the merit of the arguments of the two contestants, it is evident that if we grant Cyprian's premises we must grant his conclusions. No writings of Cyprian, except his plea against the pagans, have such power, vigor, swing, and ring, as these six

---

[21] Ep. 74 (73), 5-7.

epistles.[22] No wonder the man who wrote them dominated his age. The Roman bishops of the time are names only who would hardly be known were it not for Cyprian's writings. Besides, his premises were the premises of the Church. His main points rested deep in the ecclesiastical consciousness of his time. No one believed that a heretic could be saved, or that there was salvation outside of the Church. What was baptism then, administered there? An empty, unauthorized rite, a sacrilege. It could have no more saving efficacy than a boy's swim. Its acknowledgment as granting remission of sins in view of the repetition of a formula was both on the one hand the crassest magic, and on the other, the logical subversion of every principle held by the Catholic Church. As a true Catholic and a sharp-sighted reasoner, Cyprian went straight to the mark. If heretics had true baptism, they had remission of sins; if they had remission of sins, they had sanctification; and if they had sanctification, they had the temple of God.[23] Against that Stephen's feeble arguments broke as waves against a rock.

But what do these famous six letters teach as to Cyprian's attitude to the Roman bishop as the teacher and ruler of Christendom? Does the unity

---

[22] Ep. 69-74 (75, 69-73).   [23] Ibid. 73 (72), 12.

of the Church which goes back to Peter, and which consists in the mutual concord of forbearance and independence of the bishops, guarantee the purity of doctrine and supremacy of rule of all who chance later to occupy Peter's alleged chair? Here the great Carthaginian holds another line. Throughout his letter to Stephen there is not the slightest consciousness that he is to defer to him.[24] He gives his judgment on the question at hand, and presents his arguments, with not more feeling of dependence on Stephen's decision, than one Methodist bishop would do in relation to another in arguing for lay delegation, or an Anglican to his brother bishop against the compulsory use of the Athanasian Creed. The historical situation behind these six epistles (seven, counting the strong and remarkable letter of Firmilian to Cyprian[25]) is as different as day from night from that assumed in the Roman view. If that view is true, we are as historians in a topsy-turvy world.

Let us hear Cyprian himself on Stephen. He says that faith and religion of the sacerdotal office compel us to ask whether that priest can render a satisfactory account to God on the day of judgment who maintains the baptism of blasphemers, and he

---

[24] Ep. 72 (71).   [25] Ibid. 75 (74).

quotes Mal. ii, 12, where God says that if priests will not give glory to Him He will send a curse upon them, and will even curse their blessings. Then Cyprian launches forth in this terrible indictment of Stephen, who, according to the Roman view, is the infallible teacher of all Christians. Does he give glory to God who communicates with the baptism of Marcion? Does he give glory to God who judges that remission of sins is granted among those who blaspheme our God? Does he give glory to God who affirms that sons are born to God without, of an adulterer and harlot? Does he give glory to God who does not hold the unity and truth that spring from the law divine, but maintains heresies against the Church? Does he give glory to God, who, a friend of heretics and an enemy of Christians, thinks that the priests of God who support the truth of Christ and the unity of the Church are to be excommunicated? If glory is thus given to God, if the fear and the discipline of God is thus preserved by His worshipers and priests, let us cast away our arms; let us give ourselves up to captivity; let us hand over to the devil the ordination of the Gospel, the appointment of Christ, the majesty of God; let the sacraments of the divine warfare be loosed; let the standards of the heavenly camp be

The Great Controversy with Rome. 187

betrayed; and let the Church succumb and yield to heretics, light to darkness, faith to perfidity, hope to despair, reason to error, immortality to death, love to hatred, truth to falsehood, Christ to Antichrist. Deservedly thus do heresies and schisms arise day by day, grow up more often and more fruitfully, and with serpents' locks shoot forth and cast against the Church of God with greater force the poison of their venom; whilst by the advocacy of some, both authority and support are afforded them, whilst their baptism is defended, truth is betrayed, and that which is done outside against the Church is defended within the very Church itself.[26]

But letters were not the only weapons used against Rome. Three councils were held in Carthage, 255-6, the second with seventy-one bishops, the third with eighty-seven from the provinces of Africa, Numidia, and Mauretania, all with presbyters and deacons and laity, and reached a unanimous (in the second and third, almost in the first) conclusion to baptize all heretics and schismatics coming to them, on the ground that their former baptism was null or profane.[27] How different this from

---

[26] Ep. 74 (73), 8.

[27] On the first council see Ep. 70 (69); on the second see 72 (71); and on the third see Sententiæ Episcoporum, or the judgment of 87 bishops on the baptism of heretics (the seventh council of Carthage under Cyprian) in Migne 3, 1079-1102, and transl. in the Ante-Nicene Fathers, Edinb. ed. 13, 199 ff; N. Y. ed. 5, 565 ff.

the modern Roman theory by which no council can be held without the permission of the pope, and when held its conclusions are invalid until he indorses them. They did things differently then.

It should be said that, however intense Cyprian's beliefs and feelings on this question, so hearty was his regard for the independence of each bishop, for mutual respect and tolerance *inside the Church,* that he said distinctly that no bishop is compelled against his conscience to adopt his views or those of his compeers.[28] I prescribe to no one, says Cyprian, I prejudge no one, I prevent no bishop doing what he thinks well. Let each have the free exercise of his judgment. Charity and priestly concord must be maintained with patience and gentleness.[29] Stephen broke with him, he did not break with Stephen.[30]

---

[28] Ep. 69 (75), 17.   [29] Ibid. 73 (72) 26.

[30] On the question whether Stephen actually excommunicated Cyprian the best view is that of Ernst, "War der Hl. Cyprian Exkommuniniziert," in Zeitschrift für Katholische Theologie, 18 (1894) 473 ff., that while Cyprian was threatened with the Church ban, it never actually fell upon him. In the latter case a formal schism would have taken place between Africa and Rome, and this did not happen. From a supposition expressed in Augustine, it has been supposed by some that Cyprian later retracted his sentiments on this question. This in an article in the same journal, 19 (1895) 234 ff), Ernst also shows to be unfounded. Nor did Firmilian and the Asiatic bishops ever retract. For the later history of this baptismal strife see the article by Bonwetsch mentioned in note 2, p. 177, above.

CHAPTER XV.

THE CROWNING.

CYPRIAN had almost six years of uninterrupted activity in Carthage as a bishop, March or April, 251—June, 257. But the end was near. Valerian, an emperor of some noble qualities, who reigned 253-60, was at first friendly to the Christians, thinking thus to win them. But under the influence of his prime minister, Macrian, helped along by the vague terror of pestilence and barbarian invasions, believing that the close knit society—firmly held together by the bishops in a compact organization that nothing could shake—was a menace to the unity of the State, whose interior disunion through the Christian Church within was now meeting the disintegration threatened by Franks, Alemanni, and other tribes without—under this stimulus the patriotic Valerian determined to break up the Church *as an organization*. In June, 257, he issued his first edict to this end. There was to be no general persecution of private Christians, but the united external life of the Church was to be destroyed. All assemblies of Christians were forbidden, as well as meetings in graveyards and at the tombs of martyrs, and this by penalty of death. The clergy were to be banished and in every possible way isolated and watched.[1] The expectation was that, cut off from their leaders, the people would naturally and inevitably go back to their old gods. Dionysius, the great and pacific bishop of Alexandria, was banished, and it soon came Cyprian's turn. Genuine Acts give the story.[2]

The proconsul Aspasius Paternus. The most sacred emperors, Valerian and Gallienus, have done me the honor to send me a dispatch in which they have directed that persons not following the Roman religion must conform to the Roman ceremonies. I have, in consequence, made inquiries as to how you call yourself. What answer have you to give me? [Notice the method of trial by interrogation. Accused assumed to be guilty, and must prove himself innocent. This was the beauty of Roman law, and was followed in all the heresy trials to within modern times. Happy the accused for whom torture did not also form a part of the question.]

Cyprian. I am a Christian and a bishop. I

---
[1] Eusebius, H. E. vii, 11; Cyprian. Act. procons, 1.
[2] I follow here the version of Benson, Cyprian, 465-6.

know no other gods than the one and true God, who made heaven and earth, the sea, and all that in them is. He is the God whom we Christians wholly serve. Him we supplicate night and day for ourselves and for all men and for the safety of the emperors themselves.

Paternus. In this purpose, then, you persevere?

Cyprian. That a good purpose, formed in the knowledge of God, should be altered is impossible.

Paternus. Well, will it be "possible" for you, in accordance with the directions of Valerian and Gallienus, to take your departure as an exile to the city of Curubis?

Cyprian. I depart.

Paternus. They have done me the honor of writing to me not about bishops only, but about presbyters, too. I would therefore know from you who are the presbyters who reside in this city. [Compare the similar question of Annas to Christ, John xviii, 19.]

Cyprian. You have by your own laws made good serviceable laws against the very existence of informers. Accordingly it is not in my power to discover and delate them. However, they will be found in their several cities. [Wise answer by the sage old lawyer.]

Paternus. My question refers to this day and to this place.

Cyprian. Inasmuch as our discipline forbids any to offer themselves spontaneously, and this would also go counter to your legislation, they are unable to offer themselves. But if you search for them they are to be found.

Paternus. I shall have them found. They [the emperors] have directed further that no assemblies are to be held, and they are not to enter cemeteries. So if any one fails to observe this salutary direction he will be capitally punished.

Cyprian. Do as you are directed.

Then the Acts add: Thereupon Paternus sentenced the blessed Bishop Cyprian to be deported (*deportari*) into exile.[3]

This sentence carried with it loss of citizenship. It required special direction from the emperor before it could be inflicted, and for that reason the proconsul quoted the "præcept" of Valerian for banishing him to Curubis.[4]

Curubis (Kourba) was a little coast town fifty miles from Carthage at the back of the eastward promontory of the Gulf of Tunis. It was a paradise compared with some places to which exiles were sent.

---

[3] Acta Proc. 1. 21.   [4] See Benson. 466-7.

The Crowning.

The first night in which Cyprian slept at Curubis he had a dream of the proconsul, in which he had a premonition of his fate. It was one of those strange, circumstantial dreams which, either by laws of the soul not yet fully understood, or by some impression from above, reveals the future with lifelike vividness. Many instances of such dreams are on record, and thousands have occurred of which the record was hid in the heart of the person affected, or the matter told only to immediate friends. Some explain them as simply a coincidence, others bring in a higher law.[5]

Compared with Cyprian's lot in exile, that of nine of the thirty-one Numidian bishops who had sat with him in council was hard indeed. They were doomed to chained labor in the mines, where their treatment was so cruel that some died under it, and others were in prison. They had been beaten with cudgels, which showed that they belonged to the lower classes, and is at the same time an indication of the democratic character of ancient Christianity as to the orders in society to whom it made its chief appeal, and from whom it drew its officers. These bishops, presbyters, and others "toiled in the dark at piles of ore, choked with the smoke

---

[5] For this dream see Pontius, Vita Cypriani, 12; Benson, 469-70.

of smelting furnaces, half fed, half clothed, half their hair clipt off, sleeping on the ground." Cyprian contributed to their needs, and also sent them a letter full of praise for their sufferings and heroic endurance. He says they "advance by the tediousness of their tortures to more ample titles of merit, to receive as many payments in heavenly rewards as days are now counted in their punishments." The Lord has lifted them to the lofty height of glory, and Cyprian interprets this in noble and sympathetic spirit as but the rewards of their fidelity, seeing that they have guarded the faith, kept firmly the Lord's commands, in simplicity have preserved innocence, in charity concord, modesty in humility, diligence in administration, watchfulness in helping those that suffer, mercy in cherishing the poor, constancy in defending the truth, and judgment in severity of discipline,—a description of the model minister or bishop as valid to-day as in 257. With all Cyprian's Catholic sacramentarianism he recognized the fact that now while "there is given no opportunity to God's priests for offering and celebrating the divine sacrifices," they are all the while by their sufferings in Christ's name "offering a sacrifice to God equally precious and glorious, and that will greatly profit you in heavenly rewards."

THE CROWNING.

He then quotes Ps. li, 17, and says: "You celebrate this sacrifice day and night, being made victims to God, and exhibiting yourselves as holy and unspotted offerings, as the apostle exalts," in Rom. xii, 12. Thus it is that "our works with greater deserts are successful in earning God's good will."[6]

The answer of the martyrs of the mines throbs with loving appreciation of Cyprian, his character, his words, his example, and his gifts. By these things he has refreshed their suffering breasts, has healed their limbs wounded with clubs, has loosened their feet bound with fetters, has illuminated the darkness of their dungeon, has brought down the mountains of the mine to a smooth surface, and shut out the foul odor of the smoke.[7] O ye mutual sufferers! your spirit of love and unselfish endurance, your heroic constancy for Christ, breathes upon us across the centuries, shames our ease and listless devotion, and stimulates us to do and dare for your Master and ours!

The result of the edict of 257 did not suit Valerian or his councilors. The Church was not being uprooted fast enough. The senate had apparently so represented matters to the emperor. The latter accordingly sends a second rescript in the summer

---
[6] Ep. 76. [7] Ibid. 77.

58. It ran thus in its steel-like sharpness and
:ision:

'That bishops, presbyters, and deacons be im-
liately punished with death. Senators and men
igh rank and knights of Rome forfeit their dig-
, be deprived of their goods, and if after being
rived of their means they persist in being Chris-
s, be also capitally punished; their matrons be
rived of their goods or relegated into exile; and
: all Cæsareans [inferior officers of the fiscus,
mperial treasury, who were under the rationalis
:hancellor of the exchequer][8] who have either
fessed before or confess now suffer confiscation,
)ut in bonds, entered in the slave lists, and sent
vork on Cæsar's estates."[9]

It is evident that the author of this edict in-
led to destroy Christianity root and branch. "It
lain that the higher ranks were felt to be honey-
ibed by Christianity," which shows that with all
ittraction to the poor, Christianity was universal
:s appeal and power, "while the special provision
ut the Cæsarians illustrate the kind of employ-
its into which, as free from idolatrous taint, the

---

[8] Cæsariani were not palace officers, as often understood, nor "people
:sar's household," as Wallis translates, but under-officials of the treas-
See Benson, note 8, p. 480, whose legal and antiquarian information
urate and minute.   [9] Ep. 80 (81), 1

The Crowning.

Christians crowded." And the edict was immediately put into effect. Confiscation and executions began at once. Sixtus (Xistus or Xystus), bishop of Rome, visited a forbidden cemetery on Sunday, August 6, 258, and was then and there put to death, along with four of the seven deacons of the city.

Rumors of an impending change in policy had been rife, and to secure the facts Cyprian had dispatched messengers to Rome to find out "in what manner it had been decreed respecting us." Almost before the edict had reached Africa, Cyprian knew its exact purport. He wrote immediately to a brother bishop, Successus, who was himself soon martyred, gave him the terms of the rescript, the latest news from Rome as to its execution, and urged him and his brethren to constancy. Let these things be made known to our colleagues, he says, that everywhere the brotherhood may be strengthened and prepared for the spiritual conflict, that every one of us may think less of death than of deathlessness, and, dedicated to God, with full faith and courage may have no dread, only gladness, in this confession, in which we know the soldiers of God and Christ are not slain but crowned.[10]

The new proconsul Galerius Maximus, on re-

---

[10] Ep. 80 (81), 2.

ceiving the rescript, summoned Cyprian from his exile in Curubis to appear before him. Apparently by illness Galerius was detained at Utica, twenty miles northwest of Carthage. He ordered Cyprian to keep to his own house in Carthage until he could hear him. Strange luck that he should have had a few final days in his own beautiful gardens! Influential friends, Christian and pagan, urged him to flee. But he felt no inward promptings, and abode his time. Soon Galerius sent messengers to bring him to Utica, but Cyprian got wind of it, and preferring to die in Carthage, absented himself till the proconsul was well enough to come to Carthage itself. From this retreat Cyprian wrote his last letter of that marvelous correspondence to which we are so greatly indebted for the knowledge of the Church history and polity of the third century. This short letter is so interesting as the last word of one of the greatest and bravest of the Church's witnesses that the reader ought to have it before him in full:

"Cyprian to the presbyters and deacons and all the people, greeting. When it had been told us, dearest brethren, that the military clerks had been sent to bring me to Utica, and I had been persuaded by the counsel of those dearest to me to withdraw

The Crowning. 199

for a time from my gardens, and as a just reason was offered, I consented. For the reason that in this city in which he presides over the Church of the Lord is the place where the bishop ought to confess his Lord and to glorify his whole commons (the people) by the confession of their own prelate in their presence. But the honor of our Church, glorious as it is, will be mutilated if I, a bishop placed over another Church, receiving my sentence or my confession at Utica, should go there as a martyr to the Lord, when, indeed, for my sake and yours, I pray with continual supplication and entreaty with all my desires that I may confess among you and suffer there, and thence depart to the Lord as I ought. Therefore here in a hidden retreat I await the arrival of the proconsul at Carthage, and hear from him what the emperors have commanded concerning Christian laymen and bishops, and may say what the Lord may wish to be said at that hour.

"But do you, dearest brethren, according to the discipline which you have read from me out of the Lord's commands, and according to what you have so often learnt from my discourses, keep peace and tranquillity, nor let any of you stir up any tumult for the brethren, or voluntarily offer himself to the Gentiles. For when arrested he ought to speak, inasmuch as the Lord abiding in us speaks in that hour, who willed that we should rather confess than profess. But for the rest, what it is fitting that we should observe before the proconsul passes sentence on me for the confession of the name of God, we will with the instruction of the Lord arrange in common. May our Lord make you, dearest brethren, to remain safe in His Church, and condescend to keep you. So be it through His mercy."[11]

It was a common opinion in times of persecution that in the last supreme act of witnessing the Holy Spirit breathed a special message through the one about to suffer,[12] and it was that opinion which Cyprian voices in this letter. He naturally wanted to utter any word of that kind among his own flock. But at the last, as we shall see, the Spirit gave no sign, and Cyprian was silent. The martyrdom itself was sufficient.

Soon the proconsul arrived in Carthage, and Cyprian returned to his gardens. On September 13, 258, a chariot drove through them to the door of Cyprian's villa. In it were two principes or centurions,—one an officer of the legion and the proconsul's strator or equerry, the other a prison guard or officer. They find Cyprian at once, lift him into

---

[11] Ep. 81 (82). [12] For instances see Benson, 496.

the chariot, and drove away. His wish was fulfilled, he was to die among his people. Pontius, his deacon-biographer, tells us how his "serious joyousness" of expression was transfigured by the manful heart to lofty eagerness and almost mirthfulness.[13] "For whatsoever is begotten of God overcometh the world; and this is the victory that hath overcome the world,—our faith."[14] The proconsul was not well enough to proceed with the case. He therefore postponed the hearing till the morrow, and committed Cyprian to the safe-keeping of one of the officers, who kept him in his own house.

The next day he was taken before the proconsul. He was arraigned for sacrilege, which included every offense against religion, as the Romans understood it, and Cyprian would be the last man to deny that he was guilty of it. The proceedings were by questions and answers as before, but this time even more brief.

The Proconsul Galerius Maximus. You are Thascius Cyprianus.

Cyprian. I am.

Galerius. You have lent yourself to be a pope to persons of sacrilegious views.

Cyprian. I have.

---

[13] Vita Cypriani, 6, 15.   [14] 1 John v, 4.

Galerius. The most hallowed emperors have ordered you to perform the rite.

Cyprian. I do not offer.

Galerius. Do consider yourself.

Cyprian. Do what you are charged to do. In a matter so straightforward there is nothing to consider.

How brief, yet how fateful! The proconsul conferred with the council, as that was required in serious sentences, though he was not necessarily bound by their opinions. Then he said:

Galerius. Your life has long been led in a sacrilegious mode of thought; you have associated yourself with a large number of persons in criminal complicity; you have constituted yourself an antagonist to the gods of Rome and their sacred observances. Nor have our pious and most hallowed princes, Valerian and Gallienus the Augusti, and Valerian the most noble Cæsar, been able to recall you to the obedience of their own ceremonial. And, therefore, whereas, you have been clearly detected as the instigator and standard-bearer in very bad offenses, you shall in your own person be a lesson to those whom you have by guilt of your own associated with you. Discipline shall be ratified with your blood. [He then took the prepared tablet and read:] Our pleasure is that Thascius Cyprianus be executed with the sword.

Cyprian. Thanks be to God.[15]

The Christian multitude standing around sent up the cry: "And let us be beheaded, too, along with him." Surrounded by a guard from the Third Legion, Cyprian was led out to an open level space in the city, followed by thousands of his fellow-citizens, Christian and pagan. Many of the latter were in sympathy with him, partly on account of his shining life, partly on account of the masterly and loving way in which he showed himself the city's friend in the time of her awful visitation. In the midst of his deacons and presbyters Cyprian stood. He took off his white woolen cape, and then knelt on the ground in prayer. After this would have been the time for that word of the Lord, if any were to be given him. But he did not speak. He who had visions and occasional revelations from the Lord, as he believed (and the age of the prophets was still in the memory of the Church, and his great teacher, the Master, Tertullian, was himself a Montanist), was denied anything like that now. There was nothing that he could distinguish from his own thoughts. So he was silent. "He might disappoint

---

[15] Acta Proc. 3, 4. See Benson, 501 ff.

the people, but he would not delude them for their own good."

It was the headman's office to execute the sentence,—the *carnifex,* or *speculator,* not the centurion who had command of the party. Unnerved by the large sum given him by Cyprian, or touched by sympathy, or for some other reason, the headsman could scarcely grasp the hilt of his great sword. Noticing him tremble, the centurion immediately stepped forward, and to the kneeling and blindfolded bishop did the work with one powerful stroke.

"And so suffered the blessed Cyprian."[16]

The age of suffering unto death for conscience' sake, is, we trust, gone forever. But the last words of his last book were: "If persecution finds God's soldier in this mind, . . . and he is called away without suffering martyrdom, the faith which was ready to welcome it will not lose its reward. The wages of God are paid in good interest without any deduction for lack of opportunity. The crown is given for field service in time of persecution; in time of peace it is given to him who is certain of his will."[17]

What is the abiding significance of Cyprian?

---
[16] Acta Proc. 5. [17] Ad Fortunatum, at end.

In history he is known as the great Churchman. Full credit is given in this book to the wonderful active persistence, and even self-sacrifice, with which he defended and illustrated his High Churchly views. It is shown how they underlay all his thinking and work, and how his consistency and earnestness here even led him to his great breach with his brother of Rome, a breach which must have cost him heart-agony. And his intellectual and literary power and fertility, his piety and single-hearted devotion to Christ, and the almost preternatural insight with which he saw the real meaning and drift of the Catholic Church of his time, which found its truest incarnation in him, and the energy and enthusiasm with which he set that Church forward,—all this brought it about that the essential things for which Cyprian stood passed into the very blood of the ancient Church. In every Catholic Church of Christendom to-day, Roman, Greek, Russian, Armenian, and High Anglican,—he still lives and moves and has his being. Such world-significance is surely justification enough for treatment in a series like the present.

But from the standpoint of Christianity this is not the chief significance of Cyprian. We know that his view of the Church, all his so-called Catholic views, were narrow, mechanical, false, unscriptural. We know, too, that if he had never lived the Catholic development would not have been essentially different. He represented his age, he did not create it. Old Ignatius said in germ most of the things he said. No, the eternal lesson of Cyprian is not here. It is here: a true soldier of Jesus Christ. According to his light, according to his conscience, he served Him from his conversion to his martyrdom with utter fidelity and with brave-hearted and broadhearted love. On this account he speaks to us today, to every layman, and especially to every minister. O brother men! across the fields of history do we hear his voice urging us as true soldiers to stand in the evil day, and having done all, to stand? "Gazing down on us amid the conflict of his name," he says, "God approves those who are willing, aids the fighters, crowns the conquerors."[18] And let every minister hear himself described in the vivid military imagery of the mine-martyrs to Cyprian: "As a sounding trumpet thou hast caused the soldiers of God equipped with heavenly armor for the shock of battle, and in the forefront thou hast slain the devil with the sword of the Spirit. On this side

---

[18] Ep. 76, 4.

and on that thou hast marshaled the lines of the brethren by thy words, so that snares might be laid in all directions for the foe, the sinews of the common enemy be severed, and carcasses trodden under foot."[19]

---

[19] Ep. 77, 2.

APPENDIX I.

The Interpolations in the "De Unitate Ecclesiæ."

The famous passage in chapter 4 of the "De Unitate Ecclesiæ" is quoted above, page 169, the italicized portions being those usually designated as interpolated. In my judgment the matter is not of great importance, as the interpolations are paralleled by other utterances of Cyprian, whose genuineness has never been disputed; and as they do not and can not affect one's judgment of Cyprian's real view as to Roman supremacy, which rests on evidence demonstrably certain, therefore in the exposition of that view above I have made no capital out of the interpolations. We may therefore in a quiet spirit estimate the evidence.

There are no manuscripts of Cyprian extant which are earlier than the sixth or seventh century. The two oldest are S. and V.,—the Seguier of the library of Paris, which contains the most genuine readings and the oldest forms of words, and the

Verona, given to Charles Borromeo by the canons of Verona. Both are of the sixth or seventh century, it is not certain which. Both are without the interpolations.

The next oldest series are the Benventanus, or the Neapolitanus (date not assigned), W (Würzburg) of the eighth or ninth, some say seventh, century, R (Reginensis), and the G (San Gallensis) of the ninth. Not one of these has the addition.

Now as there was no reason in the ancient Church to leave out the words, if they were genuine, the evidence of Lower Criticism is decidedly against them. Such evidence against a disputed Bible text would be decisive.

On the same side are the following facts. A great scholar, Latini, who was working in Rome about 1550, said he had seen seven Cyprian manuscripts in the Vatican in which all these words in question were wanting. Baluze, who published his edition of Cyprian in Paris in 1726, said that he had examined twenty-seven manuscripts, not one of which had the interpolations. Bishop Fell, in his Oxford edition of 1682, used four English codices, not one of which had the italicized words. Other English texts have the post-resurrection charge to

Peter, but not the interpolated words. These are of the tenth century or later. Baluze says that the German MSS. of the eleventh century did not contain the words, nor are they found in any of the editions of Cyprian which appeared before that of Manutius in 1563, and which represent many of the MSS. now lost. See the exhaustive discussion of Benson, 200 ff. On the principles of text criticism the disputed words are doubtful. Their absence from nearly all of the oldest manuscripts is a weighty fact.

Harnack says that Pelagius I, in a letter of 558-60, first edited by Löwenfeld (*Epp. Pontiff. Rom. ineditæ.* 1885, 15.), cites the "De Unitate" 4 without knowing the interpolated sentences; while Mercati shows that the sentences are presupposed in a letter of Pelagius II about 585. They are found in Q. (Troyes codex of the eighth or ninth century), in M. (Monacensis or the Munich codex of the ninth), and in a Bodleian of the tenth or eleventh, all of which go back to one original, a lost manuscript. From this Harnack concluded in 1899 that the interpolation is not much later than the middle of the sixth century, and is of Roman origin. See *Theol. Literaturzeitung,* 1899, No. 18, 517.

The disputed words appeared first in print in the

edition of Paulus Manutius, Rome, 1563. Latino Latini did the editing in a conscientious and accurate manner. When the edition was going through the press certain changes and additions were made. "Whether," says Latini, "it was at the mere pleasure of certain persons or of set design, he knew not, some passages were retained contrary to the evidence of the manuscripts, and even some additions made." This so disgusted Latini that he withdrew both his name and his anotations from the edition, nor would the Vatican authorities allow *Ep.* 8 (2)—the Roman clergy to Cyprian—to appear in this edition, nor the famous letter of Firmilian (75 [74]). In a copy of Manutius's edition in the University Library in Göttingen there are copies of manuscript notes by Latini. Against this passage in *Un.* 4 is the note: "These words were added out of a single manuscript belonging to Virosius [clerical error for Vianesius], of Bologna, now in the Vatican, by P. Gabriel, the Poenitentiary, with the consent of the master of the sacred palace." From this interesting history it is fortunate that all the editions of Cyprian before 1563 (except the old Black Letter of 1471) were published outside of Rome,—and there had been about seventeen of them.

In the *Revue Bénédictine,* Abbaye de Maredsous, Belgium, Nos. 3 and 4, 1902, No. 1, 1903, Dom John Chapman has given a defense of the genuineness of the disputed text. There is a brief reply to this by E. W. Watson, Professor of Ecclesiastical History in King's College, London, in the *Journal of Theological Studies,* London, April, 1904, 432 ff., with a defense by Chapman in the next number of the same *Journal,* 634 ff. The reasons given by the learned Benedictine are as follows:

(1) The thought in the alleged interpolations is thoroughly Cyprianic. There was no necessity for a forgery.

(2) The style is also unmistakably Cyprianic. Watson agrees with these two points. "There is nothing inconsistent either in style or in thought in the so-called interpolations with the Cyprianic authorship,"—Watson, 433.

(3) No one living at that time could have been the author but Cyprian. (But look at the swarm of writings of that age and later which went under Cyprian's name, and of so close imitation that they deceived the very elect. Even now Cyprian experts are at variance as to some of these writings.)

(4) Not only Bede, but fathers of the fifth and even of the fourth century knew the text as inter-

polated, and from the circumstances of the origins of the interpolations, they must belong to the third century. If they went back so far they must have had a Cyprianic origin. But besides chapter 19 was changed in the copy intended for Rome. If chapter 19, why not chapter 4?

(5) The mystery of the texts is solved in this way. Cyprian wrote first a copy of the De Unitate for the congregation at Carthage in view of the threatened schism of Felicissimus. This copy was the original, and did not have the alleged interpolations. Soon after he wrote another copy to meet conditions in Rome, the schism of the confessors, Novatians, etc. In this copy he enlarged his first draft, calling attention to the Petrine chair, the necessity of union with it, etc. Now the Carthaginian copy was the basis of all the later copies. When the collections of Cyprian's writings were made it was always the Carthaginian *De Unitate* which happened to be included, not the enlarged Roman. But some manuscripts did preserve the Roman reading, which explains the existence of the enlarged chapter 4 in a manuscript nearly as old as the oldest. The Carthaginian shorter copy was that, however, which happened to be at the back of nearly all the existing manuscripts.

This thesis of Chapman's has won the weighty approval of Harnack and of the enthusiastic young Cyprian scholar, von Soden. The former says that although Chapman's view is not free from objection, it is admirably established, and, in his opinion, is correct. He says that the interpolations must belong to the fourth century, perhaps to the third, and that, moreover, Cyprian says here no more than he says elsewhere. The thought belongs to the third century. It is no mere Roman falsification. See *Theol. Literaturzeitung,* 1903, Nr. 9, 262-3. Von Soden gives his indorsement to Chapman in his "Die Cyprianische Briefsammlung," Leipz. 1904, p. 21, note, p. 202.

It seems to me, however, that Watson shows here better critical sense. This theory of two Cyprianic editions of the "De Unitate," one for Carthage and another enlarged for Rome, and that the lean kine of the former ate up the fat kine of the latter, that the African copy in a country that was later decimated by Vandal and Mohammedan, became the predominant type, so that manuscripts of Roman reading became well-nigh lost,—this theory, it must be confessed, is a large draft on credulity. Would not Rome have immense interest in circulating her edition? Would it not in time

Appendix I.

entirely supplant the scanty and far-away Carthaginian product, especially after the disappearance of the Carthaginian Church? Would not this bring it about that the shorter recension, if it survived at all, would have been considered doubtful, and even spurious?

On the supposition of later interpolations these huge improbabilities are avoided. The fact seems to be that some one in the papal interest, well versed in Cyprian, added to the "De Unitate" words and sentences taken from other places in his writings or having his stamp, in order to make him speak there much more decidedly for Peter's chair.

APPENDIX II.

CHRONOLOGICAL ORDER OF THE EPISTLES.

THIS must be made out by the most careful and patient study of the epistles themselves, with all the light that can be obtained from every other source. The old Oxford scholars, Pearson, Fell, and Dodwell, tried their hand at this, and their results appeared in the Cyprianic publications of 1682 and 1684 (See App. III). Their arrangement was accepted in the critical edition of Hartel, and is that used in all scientific work since. Migne follows the order of Baluzius, and gives besides under each epistle the numbers of Erasmus, Pamelius (1574, last ed. 1664), Rigaltius (Paris, 1648), Oxford, Leipzig, and Paris (1836). His order is that unfortunately accepted in the Ante-Nicene Christion Library (Ante-Nicene Fathers). I suggest to each owner of the latter, who is especially interested in Cyprian, to make out his own key of the Oxford-Migne arrangement by noticing the Oxford number given in a note under each epistle in the Ante-Nicene edition. Otto Ritschl subjected this question to a restudy in the most thorough fashion, as appears in his Latin Licentiate thesis, "De Epistolis Cyprianicis," Hallis Saxonum, 1885. See also his Anhang, "Die Chronologie der Cyprianischen Briefe," in his "Cyprian und die Verfassung der Kirche," pp. 238-49. He there prefers the following order (using Oxford-Hartel numbering): 63, 1, 7, 5, 6, 8, 9, 13, 14, 12, 11, 10, 21, 22, 15, 16, 17, 18, 19, 20, 24, 25, 23, 26, 27, 28, 29, 30, 31, 32, 33, 34, 35, 36, 37, 38, 39, 40, 41, 42, 43, 45, 44, 48, 46, 47, 50, 49, 53, 51, 52, 54, 55, 64, 59, 65, 56, 57, 58, 60, 62, 61, 66, 2, 4, 3, 68, 69, 70, 71, 73, 67, 72, 74, 75, 76, 77, 78, 79, 80, 81. Fechtrup's order for 5-19 is 5-7, 13, 14, 12, 11, 10, 15-19. Of the epistles in this order he places all to 12 before A. D. 250, 11th at the beginning of a new persecution, the rest in July-August, 250.

As to subject groups, 39 epistles (5-43 Oxford-Hartel numbering) belong to the first period of Cyprian's episcopate, during his absence from Carthage in the Decian persecution; 23 (44-61, 64-8) are concerned with questions which arose out of the persecution after its close and after his return; 7 (69-75) on rebaptism; the last 6 (76-81) belong to

Valerian's persecution and the closing year of Cyprian's life; the six remaining (1-4, 62, 63) are outside of the main development of the history. See "Cyprian's Correspondence" in *Church Quarterly Review*, July, 1892, 381 ff (vol. 34).

APPENDIX III.

SELECT LITERATURE.

THE first edition of Cyprian's works appeared in Rome, 1471, and an independent edition at Venice the same year. An early edition was without year or name of printer, the *editio innominata*. The sixteenth century was prolific, a sign of the awakened interest in patristic study due to the revival of learning and the Reformation. There were no less than twenty-one editions and reprints, the first being the Paris edition by Rembott, 1512, and the Basel edition by Erasmus, 1520, which last was celebrated as containing the "De Duplici Martyris ad Fortunatum," which was written by Erasmus himself and passed off as Cyprian's. The seventeenth century saw many editions, notably these, Rigaltius, Paris, 1648, and Fell and Pearson, Oxford, 1682. The most important of the later are: Baluzius (with the Mauriner Maranus after Baluzius's death) Paris, 1726, Goldhorn, Leipzig, 2 vols., 1838-9, Migne, Paris, 1844, and the careful and critical edition of Hartel, Vienna, 3 vols., 1868-71, which is that used and referred to in all books and articles on Cyprian published since 1871.

Cyprian's friend and deacon, Pontius, wrote his life (*De Vita Cypriani*) published in all editions and translations of his works. The genuine Acta Proconsularia Martyrii Cypriani appears in Ruinart, "Acta Martyrum," Amsterdam, 1713, and in von Gebhardt's "Acta Martyrum selecta," Berlin, 1902, 124-8. Modern lives, often with dissertations on various Cyprianic questions, are by Pearson, "Annales Cyprianici," Oxford, 1682, Maranus, *Vita Cypriani*, in Baluzius, Paris, 1726; H. Dodwell, "Dissertationes Cyprianicæ," Oxford, 1684; in the great collection of Tillemant, "Mémoires" IV, 76 ff, Ceilier, III, and Lumper XI; separate lives by Rettberg, Göttingen, 1831; Poole, Oxford, 1840 (superseded by Benson); Reitmeier, Augsb., 1848; Blambignon, Paris, 1861; Peters (Prof. in R. C. Episcopal seminary at Luxemburg), Regensburg, 1877 (able, but written from strictly Roman point of view); Fechtrup, Munster, 1878 (the best German life written as a separate work, but lacking in some points; see Harnack in *Theol. Literaturzeitung*, 1879, nr. 6, 125-7); Benson, London and New York, 1897. Archbishop Benson devoted thirty or

Appendix III.

forty years to the study of the life and times of Cyprian, and his book is one of the greatest monographs in Church history ever written. He has poured into notes the abundant fruits of amazing and minute learning. His book is written *con amore,* from the High Church point of view, with glowing admiration for his hero, but not without criticism here and there. It ranks with Lightfoot's Clement of Rome and Ignatius among the very greatest English patristic studies of the nineteenth century. The New York edition (from same plates) is out of print. Benson's "Catholic" standpoint occasioned the admirable brief Sir William Muir's "Cyprian, His Life and Teachings," Edinb: T. and T. Clark, 1898, 40 pp. On Benson see the *London Quarterly Review,* January 1898, 253-70,—an excellent article; *Church Quarterly Review,* London, October, 1897, 25-53; G. Kruger in *Theol. Lit.-Zeit.,* 1899, nr. 14, 413-15; F. Johnson in *Amer. Journ. of Theol.,* April, 1898, 422-6; F. H. Chase in *Critical Rev.,* July, 1897, 341-52; H. Lüdemann in *Theol. Jahresbericht,* 1897, Berlin, 1898, 195-6. Long and excellent treatments of Cyprian are also found in the "Church Histories" of Schröck, Vol 4; Neander, Boston ed., vol. I; Böhringer, "Die Kirche Christi und ihre Zeugen, oder die Kirchengeschichte in

Biographien," vol. 4, 2. Aufl. 1874, pp. 813-1039, which is often found printed separately; and Farrar, "Lives of the Fathers," Lond., 1889, vol. II, pp. 185-260.

There are many monographs and special articles, for which see the bibliography prefixed to Leimbach's article in the Hauck-Herzog *Realencyklopädie*, 3. Aufl. 1898, 367 ff., Bardenhewer, *Patrologie*, 2. Aufl. 1901, 167-175; and (for late lit.) the admirable work of Prof. Ehrhard in the *Strassburger Theol. Studien*, viz., "Die Altchristliche Literatur und ihre Erforschung von 1884-1900," 1. Abt. Freib. in B. 1900, 455-81. It will be sufficient to mention here Otto Ritschl (Son of Albrecht), "Cyprian von Carthago und die Verfassung der Kirche," Göttingen, 1885, an able and independent study, especially valuable in the second part, but specially original in the first part, in which are new combinations and results, some of which, I think, are overdrawn, as *e. g.*, his main achievement, that Cyprian's view of the Church is the result of the pressure of circumstances, the response (so to speak) to the historical situation in which he found himself, an evolution drawn out by the opposition of the presbyters, confessors, and the Novatian movement, something invented to meet contingen-

APPENDIX III.   223

cies. See the long and, on the whole, very favorable review by Zoepffel, the *Theol. Lit.-Zeit,* 1885, nr. 13, 229-304, nr. 14, 326-30; also *Th. Jahresb.* 5 (1885), 149. Carl Goetz, "Die Busslehre Cyprian," Königsb. in Pr., 1895,—an earnest scientific piece of work, corrected, however, in one main conclusion by K. Müller in "Zeitschrift f. Kirchengeschichte," 16: 187 ff K. G. Goetz, "Das Christentum Cyprians," Giessen, 1896, a careful and impartial work, but partially spoiled by a new and arbitrary terminology and method of division, on which see Lüdemann in *Th. Jahresb.* 1896, 163-4. K. H. Wirth, "Der Verdienst-Begriff in der Christlichen Kirche, II Der Verdienst-Begriff bei Cyprian," Leipzig, 1901, an excellent and exhaustive study. Hans Freiherr von Soden, "Die Cyprianische Briefsammlung," Leipz., 1904. Von Soden shows the early wide diffusion and use of Cyprian's letters. He says that numerous copies were circulated even in his own lifetime; that he himself prepared compendia of his letters (*Ep.* 27 [22]: 4); and that before Cyprian died his letters had a place in the devotional literature of the Church. The writings of Cyprian which are known to us, but which have perished, were lost at a very early date. Von Soden thinks that the oldest collection of letters was intended for confessors and martyrs, and the next collection for the strife with the heretics. "Bishop Lucifer, of Calaris, in his treatise, made use of nothing but the Holy Scriptures and the writings of Cyprian." See Tasker in *Expository Times,* June, 1904, 410.

Three English translations of Cyprian's complete works exist: (1) by Nathan Marshall, 4to, Lond, 1717; (2) by Chas. Thornton and H. Carey, in Oxford Library of Fathers, 2 vols., Oxf. 1839, 1844; and (3) by Ernest Wallis in Ante-Nicene Fathers, Edinb., 1868-9, N. Y., 1886.

INDEX

ABSOLUTION 152–5
Actor, Case of............... 50
Alexandria, Treatment of
   lapsed at......... 89, 100–1
Asceticism ... 76, 78, 144, 166–2
Atonement 155

BAPTISM—
  Regeneration in... 21, 142, 149
  By Heretics........... 176–88
  Post-baptismal Sins.... 76–7
  Sick-bed Baptism. (note) 197
Basilides of Leon, Case of.. 172
Berber Raids 122
Bible, Ancient attitude to .. 36
Bibliography, Cyprianic 219–24
Bishop—
  Office of acc. to Cyprian 41–3, 111
  Privileges of.......... 43, 165
  How elected.............. 44
  Degeneration of 55–6
  His new part in Discipline................. 80–3
  See also whole ch. 8.
  See Church.

CALLISTUS, his new decree
   as to penitents...... 81, 100
Captives, redeeming....... 123
Carthage 1–17
Certificates—
  Sacrificial 69–71
  Martyrs'...... 78–80, 85ff., 99
Christ, Doctrine of 37
Church, Doctrine of. 118–20, 148
   153–4
Clergy—
  Catholic theory of,........ 39
  Acc. to Cyprian 41–3
  As traders and laborers. 48–9
  Orders invalidated
   by grave sin 173

Cyprian—
  His training............. 18
  Conversion 20–5
  Opinion on the gods 26
  On paganism.......... 30–4
  His book against the Jews 36
  His view of Christ........ 37
  Made Bishop 38
  On Church and Ministry 39-44
  Pope 46
  Work for Discipline... 48–57
  Flees persecution........ 74
  Dealing with the lapsed 84 ff
  Returns 96
  Attitude to Novatian... 110–5
  Incites to charity in giving to captives 124–6
  To care for sick 128
  On merit of good deeds... 130
  Writes "To Demetrian." 133
  "On Mortality" 136
  "On the Lord's Prayer" 140 ff
  As a Catholic............ 147 ff
  Was he a Roman Catholic................. 163 ff
  His quarrel with Stephen,
   of Rome 176–8
  His first trial............ 190
  Banished 192
  Summoned back........ 198
  Last letter........... 198–200
  His second trial 201
  His execution 202–4
  Abiding significance ...205–7

DEAD, Prayers and offerings
   for........... 50, 159, 164
Demons, Casting out 26–8

EPISCOPATE, Carthaginian
   modeled on civil organization............. 15

INDEX.

Epistles, Cyprian's, chronological order.......... 216
Eucharist, See Supper, Lord's.

FELICISSIMUS, Schism of 92-6, 98

GODS, Origin of heathen 26, 28-9
JEWS, Cyprian on 37

LAWYERS—
  Ancient 18
  Corrupt 33
Laity—
  Place of 38
  Active in electing Bishop 44-6, 173
Lapsed—
  The (apostates to heathenism) question of.. 75 ff, 84 ff
  Final disposition of their case.............. 96, 116

MARCIAN OF ARLES, Case of 174
Merit—
  Beginning of 78
  Cyprian on........ 130, 155-8
  Treasury of...............159
Military element in Carthaginian language....... 13
Mines, Labor in, as punishment............... 64, 193
Monasticism. See Asceticism.

NOVATIAN and his movement .... 102 ff
Novatus 112-5

PÆDERASTY................ 32
Paganism—
  Moral condition of...... 22-3
  Treatment of sick.. .. 127-8
  Cruelty of 134
Persecution of Christians—
  Reasons for 58-63
  Decian .... 63 ff
  Tortures................. 135
Peter, Primacy of.......... 148
Plague of 252 ff......... 126-30

Pope—
  Title, when and for whom first used.............. 46
  Of Rome, his headship 165-75
  See Stephen.
Prayer—
  Posture in 145
  Rules for 146
  Lord's, Cyprian on..... 140 ff
Purgatory. See Dead.

SAINTS, Intercession of.... 160
Shows, Gladiatorial......... 31
Sins, Artificial Cath. distinction in............ 76 ff
Stephen, Bishop of Rome—
  His relation to two Spanish bishops........... 172
  Prompted to duty by Cyprian 174
  Opposed by Cyprian on question of Doctrine and Discipline 176-88
Suffering, Why permitted 133-8
Supper, Lord's, referred to in Lord's Prayer...... 144
  Cyprian's Views of.... 150-2, 158-9

TERTULLIAN—
  As writer 8, 11
  His significance 13-15
  His view of the ministry 39-41
  On merit 78
  On mortal sins 81
  Against assumptions of Roman bishops........ 82
Theater 8, 9, 31, 51
Trades, Ministers in...... 48-9

UNITY, Interpolations in Cyprian's book on 169, 208 ff

VALERIAN persecution 189
Virgines subintroductæ..... 52

WAR reprobated by early Christians 30

www.ingramcontent.com/pod-product-compliance
Lightning Source LLC
Chambersburg PA
CBHW062025220426
43662CB00010B/1476